HEART WHISPERER

True Stories of Help for the Heart

BY CATHY EVERITT

xulon
PRESS

Heart Whisperer
True Stories of Help for the Heart
by Cathy Everitt

Printed in the United States of America

ISBN 9781626979857

All scripture quotations, unless otherwise noted, are from one of these three translations:

New International Version (NIV) Holy Bible, New International Version. Copyright © 1973, 1978, 1984 by International Bible Society. All rights reserved throughout the world. Used by permission of International Bible Society.

New American Standard Bible (NASB). Copyright © 1960, 1962, 1963, 1968, 1971, 1972, 1973, 1975, 1977, 1995 by the Lockman Foundation. Used by permission.

King James Version (KJV)

www.xulonpress.com

The stories in this book are true. Names and details were changed to protect the privacy of the innocent and to extend mercy and grace to the guilty.

This book is dedicated to all my dear ones on both sides of the Atlantic. Thank you for your love, your encouragement and your stories.

Endorsements

"May the encouraging words of *Heart Whisperer* leap off the page and into your heart to inspire and bring about life change. Drink deep, and be filled up by these inspiring stories."

Marty Martin, Lead Pastor,
Northstar Church, Panama City, Florida

"This book will be a reflection of its author as one who loves whole-heartedly and brings the life of Christ with her wherever she goes, even to a far flung emerald isle at the ends of the earth."

Tom Burke, Senior Pastor,
Grace Christian Church, Cork, Ireland

"It is impossible to stand in the same room with Cathy Everitt and not walk out invigorated. It will be impossible to read her book and not be refreshed. Read... Refresh... Enjoy."

Roy Mansfield, Spiritual Growth Pastor,
Northstar Church, Panama City, Florida

"I have listened many times to Cathy as she spoke of God and her love for Him. Each and every time I have left those conversations hungry for a deeper relationship with Him and with a hushed heart, knowing He watched over me, my cares and my joys."

Michael O'Donovan, Pastor,
Grace Christian Church, Cork, Ireland

"Cathy is one of the most encouraging people I have ever known. I am confident her book will uplift and inspire you. "

Taylor Brown, Administrative Pastor,
Northstar Church, Panama City, Florida

Contents

Introduction

It's the desire of my heart that these stories will inspire each of us when our minds become stressed or when our hearts are hurting or discouraged for any reason. Each story tells of a challenging time in my own life or the life of one of my dear ones in America or Ireland. Every time we needed help and cried out for it, we were answered, often in an unexpected way.

As I write these words, I pray you will hear a whisper that will help your heart. After you finish reading, you might consider sharing the book with people you love. They may need to hear a heart whisper, too.

— One —

Looking Up

*H*erons are not heroes. I know this because they're a bit like roommates to me, since they're the first living creatures I meet each day. I see them on my early morning walks by the bay. Yet whenever I walk near them, they fly away like cowards, squawking their angry honking sound. I understand that I've disturbed their breakfast search of the shallow water, but why are they so afraid of me? They're taller than I am and faster, too.

The snow-white egrets are either braver or wiser. They've accustomed themselves to my daily sunrise walks here in their home and they let me walk right by, taking no notice. Why are those gray herons so afraid, I wonder?

Today something peculiar happened. Two of them stood like statues in the shallow water looking straight up into the sky. Strange, I thought, and so I looked up to see what might have caught their eye — nothing there but thick gray clouds. Were they watching the weather, sniffing the air?

Then I smiled. Today was the first day they let me walk by, unnoticed. No fear, no squawking, no flying away in anger, because they were looking up. Lesson learned, heroic herons. I'll look up, too.

— *Two* —

Just Sit There

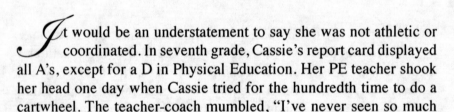

*I*t would be an understatement to say she was not athletic or coordinated. In seventh grade, Cassie's report card displayed all A's, except for a D in Physical Education. Her PE teacher shook her head one day when Cassie tried for the hundredth time to do a cartwheel. The teacher-coach mumbled, "I've never seen so much effort with so little results."

So, Cassie was not surprised a few years later when she tried to learn to water ski without success. Failure was disappointing, but not surprising. Her church youth leader, handsome Air Force lieutenant John Pense, said, "Oh, I can teach you, Cassie, guaranteed. I've taught dozens of people how to water ski."

On several Sunday afternoons throughout the summer, John tried. However, of all the fifteen or so teenagers who went on these outings, Cassie alone never succeeded, not even once.

For four consecutive summers, Cassie tried. Three other boat owners confidently assured her they knew the secrets that could make anyone succeed. She memorized their various instructions and repeated them every time she bobbled in her ski vest behind a boat.

Keep your knees bent. Straighten your arms as you come up. The boat will pull you up. Yet each time the boat tried to pull her up, she just fell forward, humiliated.

Finally, at the end of that fourth summer, no longer a teenager, Cassie received some new instructions from her brother-in-law, Jim.

"Cassie, listen to me, don't do anything. Do you hear me? Don't do anything but sit on the skis. Just sit there. Have you got that?"

Sit there? Yes! Sitting is my best skill, she thought. *I can certainly just sit there.* As she relaxed into her skis and just sat there, a glorious event occurred. The boat pulled her into a standing position and she found herself skiing all around Crystal Lake! The smile on her face stretched so wide, she wondered if her face might split apart.

Now I know what people mean when they say someone smiled from ear to ear, she thought. *I didn't know my mouth could stretch so wide and there is no way I can stop this smile. Who would've guessed that mere relaxed sitting and waiting could turn into such a fun and adventurous joyride as this?*

Throughout the rest of Cassie's life, the learning-to-ski event often returned to her thoughts. Many times in prayer, when circumstances had spiraled out of control and life's challenges seemed more than she could meet, a gentle, firm voice whispered to her heart, "Sit on the skis, Cassie. Just sit on the skis. I'm the boat and I'm the motor and I'm in control. Rest in Me, trust Me, and watch what I do *for* you and *in* you and *through* you." When Cassie learned to practice the discipline of daily sitting still in His presence, her joyful adventures began.

— Three —

Now or Never

*P*atrick and Barbara stared straight ahead, sitting in their car in the parking lot of the maternity hospital in Cork City, Ireland. They had just lost their first child to a miscarriage.

Fighting back his tears, Patrick reached for Barbara's hand and said, "We'd better praise God now or we may never be able to again." Barbara nodded, so he began to sing a song about choosing to bless the name of the Lord. Barbara sang along in gasping whispers. When they came to the line in the song that says God gives *and* takes away, her voice erupted in a gut-wrenching sob. The sound broke Patrick's heart all over again.

What an idiot I am, he thought. *I've made it worse for her by choosing this particular song.* But Barbara continued singing while she cried more softly. She knew she needed to trust God as the only giver of life. If He allowed this kind of pain, He surely would not waste it. She knew He keeps His promises and He causes all things to work together for her good.

When they told me their story, I thought about God's servant Job in the Old Testament, who said that even if God killed him, he would keep on trusting Him. Their decision to sing praises to God in their most heartbroken moment has continued to inspire me, because their choice to praise God in that moment informed the way they dealt with three more miscarriages.

Each time, they sang the same song of surrender and praise to God. Yet they now have three beautiful daughters, and when the youngest one was born, Patrick announced, "I am a blessed man, indeed!"

— Four —

The Yellow Leaf

My dear daughter, you are worried about many things, but only one thing is needed. When you do this one thing—sit at My feet and listen to Me—all those worries will drop off like dry autumn leaves from a tree.

After God whispered those words to my heart, I wrote them on a thin slip of paper, folded it and carried it in my wallet for many years.

Later, as I went for a walk, I noticed my mind worrying and fretting again. Then the amazing promise from my Heavenly Father returned to my mind. At that precise moment on that day, a lovely yellow leaf gently floated down in front of me.

I stopped walking and smiled down at the leaf on the sidewalk. I picked it up as a souvenir and looked into the tree above. I saw no other yellow leaves, only pale green ones appropriate for the month of June.

"Thank You, Lord," I said. "Thank You for this visible, tangible reminder from You. Now please, whisper to my heart, my dear Heavenly Heart Whisperer."

He did, and He does, and He will. He always will.

— *Five* —

A New Name

*B*etsy Moore Brown spoke words too horrific to believe. She told of a nightmarish childhood of imprisonment and abuse by her own deranged father after her mother died. He locked Betsy in their home and boarded up all the windows so she saw no daylight for more than two years. She told us he used her as his mistress from the time she was eight years old until she was rescued at age ten. She finally escaped by yelling through a crack in a board over a window when someone heard her and called the police. Her father was committed to a mental institution for the rest of his life.

Betsy told her story at a conference called Joy Fellowship. We began the weekend with a Friday night worship and praise service followed by Betsy's first talk. We continued the following morning with more praise and worship and then the final teaching session. She told us that for the first half of her life negative thoughts ruled her mind, telling her she was worthless and crazy just like her father. After becoming a Christian, these thoughts continued and frightened her, especially after her children were born. She feared she might someday strike out at them in a moment of anger.

She suggested to us that God has a new name for each one of us, and once she learned God's new name for her she began to act like that name and not like the names she had always called herself: *Worthless. Crazy. No-good.* She showed us story after story in the Bible where God gave one of His people a new name which branded them with a new identity: Abram and Sarai became Abraham and Sarah; Jacob became Israel.

Near the end of the last session she asked, "Are you ready to learn your new name? Bow your head and ask God to reveal to you the hurtful, negative name you have always called yourself or that others called you." The whole auditorium grew silent as we prayed. The name that came to my mind revealed what I always called myself: *Fat and Ugly*. I wept as I realized how this name summed up who I felt destined to be.

Betsy prayed, "Lord God Almighty, You are the God of new names, new beginnings, and new creations. As we again grow silent, please whisper to each lady the new name You have for her, the name You love to call her." As soon as she stopped speaking, my new name popped into my mind and I wept more deeply, but these were tears of joy and healing and overwhelming surprise. The new name my dear, sweet Jesus whispered to me began a love affair that has grown more passionate ever since. What was the new name He gave me? *Beautiful*. He re-named me *Beautiful!*

Then Betsy said, "Ladies, look up here. You now have a new name. Turn to the person beside you and say, 'I am....' and put your new name after the *am*."

Smiling through tears, I turned to the woman beside me and said, "I'm Beautiful."

Since that day, wrinkles in my face and dark circles under my eyes have increased every year. My eyelids sag so much they nearly cover my eyes now. But my name is still Beautiful because the One who created me sees me as beautiful. He's working to making me lovelier on the inside as He loves, edifies, guides and teaches me.

He's transforming me to be more like Him. I can't see it myself, but He does not lie, and I know He is changing me. Someday when I see Him face to face I may be able to see all He did on the inside to help me become more like the new name He gave me.

In the meantime, when I look in the mirror and begin to frown at the wrinkles and sagging eyelids, I remember who I am and Whose I am. This makes the corners of my lips turn upward in a sweet smile, because His Word tells me He is enthralled by my beauty. So even if

He is the only one who can see it, He is more than enough. He is the audience of one who is the only One I need to please.

He gave me a few other new names over the years, when I sat quiet and still in His presence after praising and worshipping Him. Those are our secret. His Word says He confides in those who fear (reverently trust) Him.

Will you praise and worship Him now? You might ask Him to whisper "sweet somethings" to you that are just what your hungry heart needs to hear, including your new name!

— Six —

Granite Joy

Father God, forgive me for staying in bed and neglecting my family. I would get up if I could, honest I would, but I can't. I cannot throw even one leg over the side of the bed. You say Your joy will be my strength, so give me some, Lord. Give me some sliver of joy that will strengthen me enough to get well.

Sarah fell back to sleep to dream her Alice-in-Wonderland-style dreams. Her deceased parents often appeared in these night visions. They beckoned for help but she had none to give. Waking brought relief from the urgency of the fears she felt in her dreams, but waking also brought the heavy blanket of gloom weighing her down with hopeless and anxious thoughts.

Lord Jesus, I wouldn't wish this depression onto anyone, not even an enemy. Yet I wish some people could get just a glimpse of this abyss so they wouldn't be so quick to think it's something you can just snap yourself out of.

Through the deep darkness of her months-long emotional pain and lethargy came a whispered voice. *Sarah, apart from Me, you can do nothing.*

Could that thought be from God? Added to her despair, she felt oppressed by heavy guilt for not serving God or anyone else lately. She remembered her many years of work with children's ministries — the camp-outs in the Irish countryside, where everyone got drenched with rain and mud, or infested with lice or gnats. She remembered all her striving to do better and be better and always falling short. Sometimes it seemed that "Never enough and never good enough" should be her epitaph. It had been the mantra of her mind for most of her life, but now, did she hear God saying she could just stop this exhausting striving for perfection?

As if in answer to that question, her eyes fell onto the last verses in the 11th chapter of the gospel of Matthew: "Come to Me, all you who labor and are heavy burdened and I will give you rest. Take My yoke upon you and learn of Me for I am gentle and humble in heart and you will find rest for your souls, for My yoke is easy and *My burden is light.*"

Somehow she understood that if she could trust God to carry her loads, the burden on her would lighten and be easier to bear. What a relief that would be. Could she do it? *Help me, Lord, help me just give up all this hopeless striving after perfection. Do whatever You want with me and through me. Help me trust You more.*

She read in the book of Galatians that it was for freedom Christ had set her free and she should stand firm in her freedom and refuse to be burdened again by any yoke of slavery. Slavery sounded like a good word to describe what had been oppressing her mind.

Help me, Lord. Help me live and walk in the freedom You suffered and died to give me. Can I really live and breathe freely? It seems too good to be true, but I do see joyful Christians who appear to walk in liberty. Are they trusting and resting in You to do the work through them?

Father God, I confess I've been angry with You for allowing me to go down so low. When I asked You to please not allow the doctor to give me the one prescription I dreaded, and You did let Him do it, I felt totally abandoned and betrayed. But I guess You know better than anyone how it feels to be abandoned and betrayed.

You say, Lord, that You cause everything to work for my good. Show me how this horrible pit of darkness can be turned into good. Give me the strength that comes from Your joy. I can't imagine even a pebble of joy, but someone says Your joy is as strong as granite, so give me Your granite-strong joy and restore to me the joy of my salvation.

As Sarah continued to pour out her deepest anger and hurts and disappointments to God, she began to see a sliver of light at the end of her dark tunnel of despair. Her precious teenage son played a song for her about choosing to listen to the voice of truth instead of to all the mocking, discouraging words in her head — like the thoughts that told her the light at the end of the tunnel was probably an oncoming train of disaster!

Slowly, inch by inch and thought by thought, she began to be able to participate in life again. A dear friend invited her to a new church. Hearing and singing praise songs helped bring a few more beams of light into her tunnel. Her doctor allowed her to return to the medicine that had helped her in the past and this enabled more positive thoughts to filter into her brain.

Since Sarah's worst time in the depths of clinical depression, she has helped people in similar situations. She practices a life of gratitude for her relationships — her relationship with Jesus and with her faithful husband, her son and her friends. She now thanks God often for her comfortable home and garden in Ireland. She has been lured toward the edge of the abyss, but by the grace of her loving Heavenly Father, she has stayed out of the pit of depression as she listens to His voice of truth and rests on the granite rock of His joy to strengthen her.

— Seven —

ABC's

*N*ancy sat on a metal file box in the storage closet of her classroom, praying before her students arrived. *Lord, I can't do this job. It's too hard. You've told me I can do all things through Christ who strengthens me and You've said it isn't me living my life, but You living it through me. So, will You please do this job through me today?*

I'm admitting that apart from You, I can do nothing of eternal significance, and I certainly can't help these very spoiled children from affluent homes. At every other job, my treasure box prizes were a great motivator, but at this school they just sneer at my trinkets. Help me, Lord. Do as You promise in Your Word and show Yourself strong on my behalf, as You did on the cross. Thank You for helping me get here so early today to have a time of quiet and peace before the onslaught begins. Help me, Lord. Give me patience and a peaceful spirit with my students today.

Nancy noticed her breathing slowing down and becoming deeper. Then she remembered what she'd heard at a women's conference recently. The speaker suggested going through the alphabet and praising God for at least one attribute or blessing of God using words that began with each letter from A to Z. Since the alphabet was her daily focus as a teacher of a Kindergarten Special Education class, the idea intrigued her, so she gave it a try.

Father God, I praise You for being my Abba Father, Almighty God, more than able to do and be more than I need. I praise You for beauty and bounty and blessings. Praise You, Lord, and thank You for being my Comforter and Counselor. Thank You for being delightful, and delicious when I "taste and see that You are good." Praise You that You are Emmanuel, God with us. Thank You for being Faithful Friend and Father. Jesus, You are gentle, generous, and holy and humble. Thank You for being immutable and incomparable. Praise You that You are a just Judge and Your name is Jesus.

Jesus, praise You for being a kind King and loving Lord, merciful Master, Name above all names, near to the broken-hearted, and Prince of Peace. Holy Spirit, thank You for being quick to quiet me in Your love, my Rock of refuge and Redeemer and Rescuer. Praise You for being my Shepherd and Savior from sin. Praise You that You are Truth, unshakable, undefeated and undefeatable. Thank You that You are always the victorious victor in every circumstance, wonderful counselor, wonderful way-maker.

When Nancy came to the letter X, she had to think for a while, then prayed, *Lord You are eXcellent in all Your ways, and Your promises are yes and amen. Thank You that You are zealous for Your house so that means You're zealous for me, too. Change me so I can be patient with all the students today, especially Albert. You know how his whining voice gets on my last nerve!*

After praising God, Nancy sat still a few moments longer and basked in the change that had come over the atmosphere of her tiny storage closet and over her heart. She heard the encouragement she needed: *Nancy, your day is already a success. You have done the one needful thing, to sit at My feet praising and worshipping and listening. Now look each child in the eye and make this kind of sweet connection with him or her. Let My love for them shine through your eyes and flow through your voice. Just love 'em, Nancy. I'll do the rest. A brain that feels loved and treasured can learn so much better. Give them My delicious fruit: My peace, My joy, My love, My patience and gentleness.*

Nancy opened the storage room door and looked at her classroom with new eyes. She smiled as she put each child's journal on the desks. When she stamped the date onto the first blank page of each journal, she smiled at their entries from the day before.

Albert had only scribbled with black crayon, as usual. So she used a yellow crayon to make a sun at the top of his new blank page and drew a smiling face on it and wrote "I love you, Albert. I feel happy today. Please draw a picture to show how you feel today." She knew she would need to read this to him, but maybe the moment of extra attention would help start his day a little bit better. If he felt like scribbling with a black crayon again today, that was okay. She had those kinds of days herself.

But not today. Today was already a success and it was barely 7 AM.

— Eight —

No Matter What

$\mathcal{L}$ana loved competition. She and her friends at the gym in Cork City kept a record of who swam the most laps and jogged the most miles on the treadmill. They played frantic card games where no one took turns and lightning reflexes and speed determined the winner. She displayed good sportsmanship whether she won or lost, but she seldom lost. When she did, she often charmed her way into an immediate rematch.

She even worked hard to excel as a homeowner. She kept her home and garden looking worthy of a magazine photo shoot at all times, taking pride in the accolades she received as a cook and hostess. She also loved going to battle for anyone who suffered mistreatment or injustice. Yet when it counted the most, God told her to be quiet and let Him compete and battle for her.

As many rumors do, it started with a misunderstanding. Someone she loved told a rumor that many people believed. She ached to reveal the truth, to defend herself and scream out loud, "I'm innocent!" However, to explain the circumstances would require revealing intimate secrets of people she loved. When she cried out to God, she knew He said, "No, don't say a word. Don't defend, don't explain. I've got this."

So, when friend after friend confronted her about the shocking news, and a few said they couldn't remain friends with her, or demanded an explanation, Lana's answer was always the same, "I'm just going to love *you*, no matter what." This ended the questioning, but it was the hardest thing she ever did. She found comfort in knowing the Bible said everything now hidden will someday be revealed. She prayed for God to vindicate her, since she couldn't defend herself without hurting others.

I was a bystander during all of this. I had heard the rumor but couldn't believe it. Whenever I prayed and asked God what to do, He seemed to whisper, as He so often does, "Just love her." So I did. But it felt like there was a big elephant in the room whenever we were together. I had so many questions, but when I prayed, I knew it was not my place to ask, not yet. *Lord,* I prayed, *I'll just love her, like You said. No matter what she may or may not have done, it could never compete with the things I've done that You've so generously forgiven me for. Show me how to be honest but leave all the questions and answers to You.*

After two years of my wondering, Lana shared her story with me. It filled me with admiration that she would endure slander to protect others and I thanked God to have a friend with so much strength. I knew how hard it must have been for a "take-charge" person to stay quiet and let go and wait for God to straighten things out, but she did.

And He did. He "got it all sorted," as the Irish say. God showed her that He is the only One who can unravel the problems that seem like tangled up fishing lines in our lives. In Lana's case, friendships were restored and she learned how to quiet her competitive heart and to trust God to take care of her, no matter what.

Nine

The Combat Boot

I wanted to die. My heart ached so much from emotional pain, rejection and fear that it felt as if a soldier wearing combat boots was pressing one of his feet down hard onto my chest. Each breath brought painful effort and I wished my breathing would just stop. But how could I give up on life when I had my precious three-year-old son depending on me?

My friend Susan came over with ice cream to try to console me, but I looked at the carton and gagged. For the first time in my life, there was no comfort food that could offer any hope of relief.

What caused this excruciating pain? My husband of seven years had just dropped by to take our son to spend the night for the first time at his new bachelor apartment.

This is real, I thought. *My husband has really moved out. How can my child grow up in a broken home? How can my heart keep beating when it feels as if this 200-pound something or someone is pressing down on it?*

After Susan left, I lay face-down on our pale green carpet and cried aloud to God, "Help me! How can this be happening when so many people have been praying with me that this would not happen?" I got up and sat on our sofa and began to read from the Bible where I had found relief in less shattering times. I turned to a favorite portion and hungrily read several pages, struggling to focus on the words.

One verse "jumped off the page" as if my name was written in it for exactly this moment. The heavy combat boot lifted off my chest and my heart flooded with comfort and hope.

Here is the life preserver my Heart Whisperer gave to me on that desperate day, like a personal note of salvation to rescue me: "'The mountains may be removed and the hills may shake, but *My* loving kindness will not be removed from you, and My covenant of peace will *not* be shaken,' says the Lord who has compassion on you" (Isaiah 54:10, NASB).

My faith somehow began to change from faith in something happening—or not happening—into faith in the One and Only One who will never change or let me down. I realized anything can happen, even the most dreaded things. Hurricanes, tornadoes, floods, fires, heartbreaks, betrayals and break-ups happen. No one escapes life without pain, and emotional tsunamis can destroy just as surely as those from the ocean. Yet my Abba Father's love, compassion and powerful, miraculous peace are always available when I ask.

The more desperate I am when I cry out for Him, the closer He feels to me. In the twenty-six years since He sent me that personal love note in Isaiah 54:10, the deep truth of it has been proven again and again. Many hills have been shaken and many good and bad mountains have been removed, but God in His kindness has always loved on me whenever I cried out to Him for help.

Won't you let Him love on you? He's waiting for you with open arms and with love notes from His Word. His name is Jesus.

— Ten —

Heart Whisperer

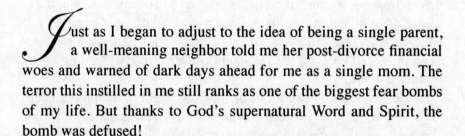

*J*ust as I began to adjust to the idea of being a single parent, a well-meaning neighbor told me her post-divorce financial woes and warned of dark days ahead for me as a single mom. The terror this instilled in me still ranks as one of the biggest fear bombs of my life. But thanks to God's supernatural Word and Spirit, the bomb was defused!

Some people say worrying is normal and unavoidable. Yet God's Word tells us hundreds of times to not be afraid, and to be anxious about nothing. One of my favorites is the one where Jesus assures us the very hairs on our head are numbered.

As I prayed for God's peace to replace the fears of future financial problems, I was brushing my hair and noticed the usual stray hairs on the bathroom sink. This reassuring thought from God's Holy Spirit came into my mind and I knew it was an answer to my prayer.

Cathy, after that hair fell onto the sink, I still know the exact number now remaining on your head. If I am that mindful of your hair, how much more faithful will I be to provide all your needs from My endless, unlimited supply?

Many years later I can confirm He has done just that. I never lacked any necessity and neither did my child. God used my son's dad, my jobs and many other resources to provide all we ever needed. The Bible gives a funny statement in Psalms 50:10 when

God says He owns "the cattle on a thousand hills." What an under-statement, since He also owns all the millions of hills and mountains on earth, too!

A friend of mine in Ireland, a city girl, once acted as a "cow whisperer" to convince some cows to stop blocking our narrow road in the Irish countryside. This didn't surprise me because I had already witnessed her perform as a dog and cat whisperer when caring for her own or others' pets who became distressed for any reason.

When I have become distressed or burdened with fear, guilt, grief, loneliness, or anything less than an abundant life of peace and joy, the Almighty God of the Universe has intervened as Heart Whisperer to my heart. He sent His Son to suffer and die to make this intimate relationship possible by paying for my sins. So, if He would do such a thing as that, why would He withhold comfort and courage when needed? Who could be better to heal and comfort my heart than the One who created it and caused it to start beating in my mother's womb?

Does your heart need soothing, healing or strengthening? Listen. He's whispering. If you can't hear Him, try reading the following verses aloud in a quiet place with no distractions. Read until you notice your breathing becomes deeper and your mind becomes calmer. I believe Jesus provides the "balm of Gilead," the ointment that soothes the most painful hurts.

Read in your Bible where it says He longs to be gracious to you and He rises to show you compassion. Read the passage where He tells us, "Call to Me and I will answer you and tell you great and mighty things you do not know." Check out this one: "As a father has compassion on his children, so the Lord has compassion on those who fear (reverentially trust) Him."

"Can a mother forget the child nursing at her breast? Even these may forget you but I will never forget you!"

"Do not fear, for I am with you. Do not anxiously look about you for I am your God. I will strengthen you, I will uphold you. Surely I will uphold you with My righteous right hand."

"I will give you beauty for ashes and the garment of praise for a spirit of heaviness." "Many are the afflictions of the righteous but the Lord delivers him from them all." (Don't let anyone tell you that you aren't righteous. If you have put your faith in Jesus and asked for His forgiveness, you're cleansed by His blood. The Bible says He has made you to become "the very righteousness of God in Christ" and that He has given you "the *gift* of righteousness and the *abundance* of grace!")

Have you fallen or failed and don't want to try again? You might meditate on this verse: "The righteous man falls seven times but rises again."

Are you worried or fearful? Perhaps write this verse on an index card to keep on your mirror: "When my anxious thoughts multiply within me, Your comforts delight my soul!"

You could read the Song of Songs by Solomon when you're feeling unloved. It tells of God's passionate love for you and says His banner over you is love. You are "His beloved" who will come out of the wilderness leaning on your Beloved. It's amazing how differently I behave when I remember with gratitude how unconditional and how passionate His love is for me!

Jesus said, "My peace I leave with you." Jesus lives inside each believer and He's the Prince of Peace, Almighty God, King of kings and Lord of lords. That means to me that He's the Boss of everything and His peace is always available for us.

He promised to keep in perfect peace the one whose mind is focused on Him because she or he trusts in Him. He says, "Come to Me all you who are weary and heavy-laden and I will give you *rest*. Take My yoke upon you and learn from Me for I am gentle and humble in heart and you will find rest for your souls. For My yoke is easy and My burden is light."

The apostle John wrote a letter near the end of the New Testament that tells us God's commands are not burdensome. His commands are to love God and love other people. He doesn't even expect us to try to love unselfishly in our own frail strength. When we cooperate, He empowers us to do it, so we don't have to groan and grit our teeth.

When my to-do list grows too long and I notice I'm pushing myself to exhaustion or feeling defeated or overwhelmed, I give a sigh of relief when God reminds me of this verse from the book of Micah: "He has told you, oh man, what is good. And what does the Lord require of you, but to act justly, to love mercy and to walk humbly with your God?"

He's teaching me that "to walk humbly" with my God means to do the one needful thing — let Him love on me. Since I can't accomplish anything of eternal value unless motivated by His unconditional love, I have to get filled up by Him every day. On the most challenging days it's necessary to get frequent refills, but He never runs out on me!

And guess what? If I focus on Him, walking in step with His whispers, the part about "love mercy and act justly" gets done, too, by His strength working through me. So that shortens the list down to just the one needful thing again — listen to the Heart Whisperer.

Choice

No early morning brisk walk today.
This day she sits quietly here by the bay
To watch the world waken while she sips her Earl Grey.

Dragon-flies' herky-jerky flight patterns
Contrast with Egret's dignity and grace with no concerns
For rushing and stressing. And so, she learns

That the choice is hers as she begins this day:
Which moves will she make when she leaves the bay?
Choose the herky-jerky, or walk with grace along the way?

— *Eleven* —

April's Story

I liked April as soon as I met her. She kept us laughing until we were "drinking our tears" at the home of our mutual friend Mary, who lived at the top of one of the steepest summits in hilly Cork City, Ireland. April had just told us about losing twenty-five pounds of weight and now she described her efforts to give up smoking. "But now I've turned into a shopaholic," she said. "Look at the diamond ring I've just bought on credit. If I keep working at this jewelry store I'll soon be in the poor house."

Her thick Cork accent, combined with a lightning fast rate of speaking, made it fun and exciting to listen to her. If my mind wandered for even a second, I might miss the next thing she said that sent the room full of women into gales of laughter. During the course of her monologue she mentioned the "twenty-six tablets" she used to take.

This puzzled me. She looked several years younger than I, and I had never met anyone who took more than one or two prescription medications unless they were elderly, or a veteran of an organ transplant. When she met me later to tell me her story, it reminded me of the miracles of Jesus recorded in the New Testament— drastic transformative healing!

We met in her favorite vegetarian restaurant by the River Lee. She told me she spent many years almost never leaving her bedroom in her parents' home. She battled irrational fears of everything outside that one room. She even feared stepping on cracks in the floor of the hallway, so she straddled them whenever she needed to make her way to the bathroom. Thoughts of suicide lured her often, while the fear of death usually prevented her from acting on those thoughts. Yet when the pain of living exceeded the fear of dying, she gave in to the lure and attempted suicide.

April ended up spending two and a half years as an in-patient in three different institutions for people with acute mental illnesses. The doctors discharged her with twenty-six tablets prescribed for her various mental ailments. Some of the drugs were intended to offset the side effects of some of the others. She also received an anti-psychotic injection twice a month. She needed to use the psychiatric services for almost twenty years and she told me her career as a mental patient made her feel she was no good for anything else.

April said she had always believed in God, but had been terrified of Him, too, and she had no knowledge of the Bible. Her cousin in America, a "born-again" Christian, told her about the power of singing praises to God.

One day, while working in the jewelry shop, she began to think of things she was able to do, like walk, talk and hold down a job. Her feelings of gratitude began to multiply. For no apparent reason she felt a strong urge to sing praises to God but didn't know how.

She rang several churches in the city and asked if they sang praise and worship songs. None of them did, although a few said they sang hymns. After calling dozens of numbers in the phone book, she found the number of a "born-again" Christian Church. The young man who answered the phone, Barry, said they sang praise and worship songs all the time and that he and his wife would meet her at the front door if she wanted to give it a try.

April went to the church the next Sunday. Instead of staying in her room when not at work, she began going to church every Sunday morning and every Tuesday night. She said she felt at home from the first time she went there. She began to read the Bible and to understand what Jesus had done for her by taking all the punishment for sin. Before long she invited Christ to be her Lord and Savior and was baptized about six months later.

With the help of her physician, she came off the anti-psychotic injections, and twenty-five of the twenty-six medications. She grew confident in what God could do and watched as He continued to perform huge miracles in her life. She stopped using the mental health services, and went to college as a forty-year-old.

Through a fellow college student she heard about an organization that trained people to be peer advocates for mental health patients. She began training and became a volunteer advocate, working in the hospitals where she had been a patient herself.

April's family members were stunned at her transformation. Her parents and sisters watched her change from being extremely shy, introverted, depressed and fearful into an independent, friendly, chatty, open-minded and open-hearted woman. She spoke with transparency and eagerness about what God had done in her life because no one else could have changed her.

Her family knew she had been to most of the psychiatrists in Cork City, as well as to many of the psychologists and counselors. She told them that until she met the living Christ, nothing filled the huge gaping hole in her heart and life. Her need for excessive shopping, for self-help books, and for "stuff" continued to decrease and disappear as God, in His timing, filled the empty void with His love, support, guidance and hope. There could be no denying April was a new person. She laughed out loud with exuberance like no one else in her family. She glorified God. She became involved in service to other people through her church and her volunteer job, and she felt her life had meaning and purpose now.

Her family couldn't understand what was happening. Could this be the same April? At first she had been afraid to tell them she was going to a "born-again" Christian church, something still unusual in the Republic of Ireland at that time, but soon she invited them along. Her mother started praying with her on the phone every night and before long she, too, surrendered her life to Jesus Christ. April's mom began to rely on Christ alone for salvation instead of on her religious rituals.

April ended this phase of her story by using a new word she invented. "God is still in the business of 'miracle-izing.' I'm living proof!"

— Twelve —

April Continues

$\mathcal{E}$ach summer when I returned to Ireland, April and I met again at her favorite vegetarian restaurant by the River Lee. She brought me up to date on her relationships with her parents and sisters and said the volunteer job working with patients in the mental health system would turn into a paid job. She was "over the moon" with excitement about this.

Watching her grow closer to God and her family, especially her mother, was one of the delights of each trip to the beautiful Emerald Isle. The more I learned of Ireland, the more I discovered and treasured the greatest jewels within this emerald — the people.

As she usually did, April asked me about my elderly parents, then my son and my sisters. She remembered their names and details she'd been praying about for me. She made me laugh as she poked fun at herself and her remaining quirks, but from what I observed she was at least as mentally stable as everyone else I knew. Maybe more so than some of us!

One day April called and said she needed to learn to use a computer for her new job, but she was terrified of computers and convinced she could never learn to use one. Our friend Sarah and I met her for lunch in City Center. We reminded April of all the miracles God had already accomplished in her life and told her that learning computers would be a small miracle compared to those! Ever since our lunch, she has often reminded me of what we told her that day, that everyone who trusts in Jesus can do whatever they need to do, because of the power of the One who lives within.

Now April is a whiz at using computers in her full-time paid job as a mental health advocate. Since she has been through the system as a mental patient herself, she is uniquely gifted to understand her clients in an effective and compassionate way.

One summer April admitted to me she had been abused as a young child but kept it hidden as a form of self-preservation. She was convinced she would never be the marrying type and joked about not wanting to "draw trouble on herself." However, God had other plans for her, good plans. Through a friend from church, she met a man from West Cork, a kind and gentle man.

In April's mind there was no idea of even the possibility of any kind of relationship. This kind-hearted, generous man spent five years sending e-mails to April to ask her out, but she never received the e-mails. She said she believes this was a work of God to keep her remaining friendly with Victor, because if she had received them at first, she might have run back to therapy with the fright!

Yet, after God had worked more healing inside April's heart, in His timing, she met up with this dear, shy man one day. He had waited patiently for five years and on this day he said he felt a physical push to his backside to make the move to ask her out. So he did.

Over time, April's heart began to melt for this soft-spoken, kind, respectful man, and he started attending church to be with her. He began hearing the Word of God, reading the Bible for himself, going to Bible study groups, and seeking God with all his heart. He asked all the hard questions as he studied God's word to find Truth. He gave his life to the Lord and was baptized. Two years after their first date, after almost a lifetime of bachelorhood and spinsterhood, when they were 47 and 48 years old, April married the godly man God had planned in advance for her. They are living proof that nothing is impossible with God.

— Thirteen —

Ultimate Survivor

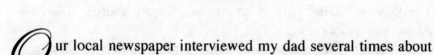

$\mathcal{O}$ur local newspaper interviewed my dad several times about his experience at Pearl Harbor when it was attacked in 1941. One year, a columnist began by writing, "Ronnie Everitt was able to find humor in the midst of horror."

When I read this statement I laughed and suggested to Dad it sounded like a motto for our family – we try to find humor even in the most difficult times. It occurred to me that whenever any kind of bomb falls into my life, my father could be an inspiring example of how to be a survivor.

I always enjoyed hearing my dad's version of "The Day of Infamy." He said he had just eaten breakfast and sat in the day room looking at a *Popular Mechanics* magazine. He was stationed at Hickem Field, the Army airbase at Pearl Harbor. While he read, on that morning of December 7, the building began to shake.

At first, his sergeant said "Don't worry; it's only the Marines on maneuvers again." A split second later, the sergeant jumped up and yelled, "No, no, this is Sunday, the Marines don't do maneuvers on Sundays!"

Their superior officer, a lieutenant, panicked and ordered everyone outside into the open for roll call — not a safe idea with bombs and bullets falling from the sky.

The sergeant said to the lieutenant, "Excuse me, Sir, but if we need any Boy Scouts, we'll call you later," and the sergeant told the men to take cover. When there was a pause in the shelling from the enemy planes, he ordered the men to run and man the anti-aircraft guns. Dad said the sergeant never got in trouble for rebelling against the lieutenant because the lieutenant probably didn't want to advertise his own panic.

When my parents were in their late seventies, we filmed an interview with them so their grandchildren could have a record of their stories of life during the Depression and the Second World War. One of the questions was, "What has been the most significant event of your life?" Without hesitation my father said it was being at Pearl Harbor the day it was attacked. However, just a few years after the video interview, a new bomb dropped into his life which made The Day of Infamy pale in comparison — our mother developed Alzheimer's disease.

Although many people helped my parents endure that challenge — their six daughters, grandchildren and sons-in-law, church and neighborhood friends, relatives near and far and the Council on Aging's Nixon Respite Center – the brunt of the challenge was on our dad. He faced and survived this like the ultimate survivor he was, with courage, resourcefulness, faithfulness and two life-long passions, one for hard work and one for learning new things. He educated himself on the disease and on other new things like learning to use the computer and the internet. Yet, in spite of his natural skills and abilities, he came to the end of himself and cried out to God in desperation.

After listening to sermons his whole life, he said he finally accepted for himself the free gift of salvation from Jesus. He discovered relief and help in his daily challenges through an intimate two-way relationship of communicating with God through the Bible. The Bible changed from being just a holy history book and became a daily love letter from His Creator to help him through each challenging day as a caregiver. He asked to be baptized as a new believer just before his 81st birthday.

One of the greatest tools in my dad's toolbox of survival skills was always his sense of humor. In my memories I can see him now throwing back his head to laugh with deep appreciation for a good joke or story. His brother was especially gifted at making Dad laugh, and I always counted myself a success if I could say something to make him toss his head back with laughter in the same way my uncle could.

Throughout the many stressful and hopeless moments of our mom's losing battle with Alzheimer's disease, Dad could still find something to laugh about on most days, usually at himself. He modeled the truth of his son-in-law's plaque that said, "Blessed is the man who can laugh at himself, because he will never cease to be amused." He demonstrated that laughter really is good medicine, and he showed us that even life's most difficult challenges can be handled by trusting in God for help and by looking for humor in the midst of horror.

— *Fourteen* —

Diagnosis

My heart pounded as I listened to the devastating news coming through my phone. My sister tried to keep an upbeat tone in her voice, but I recognized the pain beneath the surface as she spoke. She finished the phone call by asking me if I'd go with her to a conference about Alzheimer's, now that our mom had received the official diagnosis.

"Okay, Linda. The more we know, the better we can all cope with this. Maybe they'll give us some shred of hope, don't you think?"

Linda couldn't answer and just said, "Gotta go. Love you."

I put down the phone and sat at the kitchen table. I stared at the swirled designs in the tabletop. They reminded me of what I'd read about Alzheimer's disease causing tangles inside the brain. I began to weep. *Why her, God? They say there's no hope for this disease. Help her. Dear God, help all of us.*

Words from a poem by Emily Dickinson popped into my thoughts. "Hope is the thing with feathers/That perches in the soul/And sings the tune/Without the words/And never stops at all." *But there is no hope with Alzheimer's — none. Dear Lord,* I prayed, *You are the God of hope, so please give us some.*

I turned in the Bible to a verse I'd recently discovered, Romans 15:13. "May the God of hope fill you with all joy and peace as you trust in Him, so you may overflow with hope by the power of the Holy Spirit."

Lord, how can I be filled with hope about something that has no hope? Show me how to trust You and show all of us the way through this.

I thought about how God parted the Red Sea to let His people walk through on dry land to the other side. What kind of miracle could get my family through this ocean of fear and pain? I turned up the volume on the kitchen radio when I noticed a song about God lifting us up during troubles.

After the song ended, a Bible teacher's program began. I couldn't believe what I heard when the announcer said he would be teaching about hope. *God, You are so good to me. I don't even usually have the radio on at this time of day.*

I got a pen and pad out of my kitchen junk drawer so I could take notes, but I didn't need a written record for one of the statements he made. As soon as I heard it, the words etched themselves into my brain. "In the Bible, the word 'hope' means a confident expectation of good."

Confidently expect good, Lord? How can we confidently expect good when our mother has Alzheimer's? There can't be any good in that!

Then a precious soothing whisper dropped into my heart: *From Me, Cathy, you can always expect good. I have never allowed anything in your life without bringing good out of it. Watch for the good. Let the eyes of your heart be enlightened so you can know the hope of your calling and the glorious riches of your inheritance. I'm your inheritance. I am your treasure. Rest in My arms of love and watch Me work. Trust Me. Your mom is safe with Me.*

The comfort of the Lord changed the very atmosphere in the room. Just a few minutes earlier I had sensed only a heavy, oppressive fear and dread. Now, in their place I felt the thing with feathers, singing to my heart a tune that soothed and healed. I remembered other crisis times in my life and how God brought beauty, and good things, from what had seemed hopeless before.

Throughout *most* of the nine years after our mother's diagnosis, I confidently expected good. I watched for it and rejoiced in it. My entire family grew closer than any of us ever dreamed possible and we described it as "circling the wagons" against the enemy of Alzheimer's. Each of her six daughters contributed an essential piece to the team, and for two years I had the honor of serving as captain when I moved into our parents' home to be caregiver along with my dad. During this time, my mother and I gained an intimate relationship we'd never had before, and I've treasured those precious memories ever since.

Only in the last year of our mom's life did we pray for the end to come. As it finally came, her daughters and granddaughters circled her bed and sang together, "Soon and very soon, we are going to see the King."

Yes, the King. My mother was with Him now, waiting for her dear ones to join her. There could be no greater good than that.

— Fifteen —

The Secret Place

—»«—

*J*ean's mother was appalled when she learned the name of the hospital where they planned to take her four-year-old grandson for surgery. "Jean! That hospital is in the worst neighborhood in Philadelphia. Your cars will be vandalized if you park them on the street."

"I know, Mom, but that's where the best pediatric neurosurgeon in the state practices, and you know I researched all the possibilities. Will you keep Allison a while longer for us?"

"Of course we will, Dear, for as long as you need. I'm praying for all of you, and Allison will have a great time with us, so don't worry at all. Be careful in that neighborhood, and park your car in the hospital's guarded parking lot."

Jean thanked God for her mother. At least she wouldn't need to worry about *one* of her two children. *And Lord*, she prayed, *help me totally trust You to take care of little Adam throughout this ordeal tomorrow instead of fearing and worrying. Help me remember the whole 91st chapter of Psalms, so I can pray it over and over no matter where I am. You say if we hunker down and settle in Your secret place, You will keep us safe. Help me praise and worship You now in this secret place of Your presence. Thank You that You give Your angels special charge over Adam and over all our family.*

The next day, after parking their car in the hospital parking lot protected by razor wire fencing and a security guard, Jean and her husband carried little Adam into Admissions. At only four years old,

49

he was facing spinal surgery to remove a tumor deep inside one of his thoracic vertebrae. It lay tangled within the nerves, and removing it could mean permanent paralysis, according to all the experts.

The pediatric neurosurgeon had told them they had only two options. If they left the tumor alone it would most likely continue to grow, causing paralysis and much worse. But removing it could also cause paralysis. Talk about being between a rock and a hard place! Yet Jean and her husband knew a Healer. She knew He had shown them a verse in the book of Exodus that said, "I am the Lord who heals you" (Exodus 15:26).

During the four-hour surgery, Jean prayed God's own words that had been comforting her during all the weeks of testing and doctor visits. She had learned in a Bible study group that praying God's Word increased her own faith and it accomplished great things in God's kingdom. It combined two offensive weapons, the Word of God and prayer, against whatever challenges were fighting against her. One Bible teacher said it was like strapping two pieces of dynamite together.

Lord, You say You'll give me peace and rest when I settle and dwell in Your secret place, she prayed. *I say of the Lord, He is my refuge and my fortress, my God in whom I trust. I know You will save Adam from this trap and You will even protect him from deadly pestilence, which to me means You will protect him from any infection that might try to attack him during or after this delicate surgery.*

Lord, Your truth and Your faithfulness are a shield to our whole family right now. Even if ten thousand fall at our side, You will lift us up; You will deliver us because You have set Your love upon us and because we know You and trust You. You say You will answer us when we call to You. I am calling on You now, Lord. Show Your mighty power to the doctors and nurses!

An hour earlier than expected, Adam's surgeon entered the waiting room, shaking his head. Was this a good sign? Then Jean noticed he was smiling, too. His first words confirmed what she had hoped and prayed would happen.

"It's a miracle, Jean, a miracle. As soon as we got down to the level of the tumor, it just popped out on its own, like a bubble. I have no explanation for it. The most difficult part of the procedure was going to be cutting it out from all the nerve tissue, but it just popped up and out, like when someone blows a bubble out of their mouth with bubble gum!" The surgeon chuckled and continued to shake his head as if he were trying to clear it.

Then he added, "I'm going to report this, of course, but if I didn't have witnesses to confirm what happened in there, they would lock me up as a mad man. You told me you were praying for a miracle and Lady, you got one!"

So, no paralysis! Praise You, Jesus, my God who heals! Thank You for this secret place in Your presence, where I can go for help and protection. Even in this rough neighborhood with crime and danger all around us, Your nearness and Your powerful Word provided a secret place of safety and healing power!

— Sixteen —

Hospital Trauma

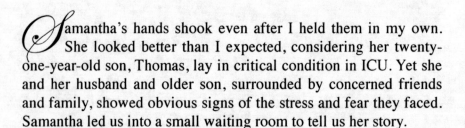

*S*amantha's hands shook even after I held them in my own. She looked better than I expected, considering her twenty-one-year-old son, Thomas, lay in critical condition in ICU. Yet she and her husband and older son, surrounded by concerned friends and family, showed obvious signs of the stress and fear they faced. Samantha led us into a small waiting room to tell us her story.

Their phone rang at 2:30 on that Sunday morning to bring the news their younger son had been in a serious car accident—caused by a drunk driver who crashed into their car and killed Thomas's best friend, who was driving. The drunk driver received only minor injuries. Thomas fiercely fought for his life while hundreds of friends and family prayed for a miracle. Thomas's father saw him in the ER first, and tried to stop his wife from coming behind the curtain because of what she would see, but he couldn't even slow her down. She discovered much later that the drunk driver was behind the curtain right beside them.

Samantha said she felt the overwhelming urge to call out to God. She took the trembling hands of her weeping husband and older son and prayed: *Dear Lord, please bring Your angels to surround Thomas. Please give the doctors what they need, and the knowledge to repair everything broken in him. Give him the strength to come back from this, no matter what the injuries. Help him feel safe knowing You and Your angels are always with him.*

They discovered God had already positioned an angel in the car that night to help Thomas. The passenger in the front seat was an EMT who tried in vain to keep the driver alive while also holding Thomas's airway open.

The hospital staff instructed them to move into a small waiting room until the doctors working on Thomas could get him stabilized. When one of the many doctors finally came in to give them a report, his face spoke bad news before he opened his mouth. He told them Thomas sustained extensive and grave injuries. The only prognosis he could give them was to wait and see. Wait and see about the bleeding on the brain, the swelling in his brain, his lacerated bladder, torn liver, broken pelvis. Wait and see about his lungs, which had been re-inflated with chest tubes inserted, wait and see about the broken ribs and broken facial bones "too numerous to count."

At about 5:45 AM, he was transferred to the Neuro-ICU where the nurses evaluated him and cleaned up his wounds. His nose and ears leaked massive amounts of blood which made his face frightening to see, and his left eye was swollen shut. Samantha said she could see he was frightened and had no idea what had happened or what was happening around him now. They tried to reassure him, and she said God strengthened her enough to sing to him "You Are My Sunshine," his favorite song when he was little.

After Samantha brought us up to date on the story so far, we prayed with her. We went back into the hallway where Thomas' friends and co-workers waited, spoke a few words to her husband and older son, hugged them, and drove back to our home two hours away. After three more days, she reported him out of the woods at last, but facing many weeks and months of recuperation.

Thomas endured eight days in ICU, several surgeries, seven days in the orthopedic wing of the hospital and then ten more days in a rehabilitation hospital. After all this came more therapy. Some of his injuries were permanent, and every day when he sees the big scars on his body, it reminds him of his best friend who died in the crash.

When I asked Samantha what sustained her family through this frightening ordeal, she gave glory and thanks to God. She said there were many times when she and her husband had no strength to continue their round-the-clock vigils while still working to make a paycheck. Yet God strengthened them to do it, and Thomas firmly insists God saved his life the night of the accident.

In the first early days of uncertainty, when fear took hold of her, Samantha learned to survive by taking slow, deep breaths as she talked to Jesus and told Him her every fear. She thanked God for the strength and support of her older son and her husband, who grew closer to one another, to Thomas and to her than they had ever been. Before this happened, she never knew the power God could give them as a family, and their closeness to one another has continued to grow.

It's been said we don't know what we have 'til it's gone. Samantha and her family came so close to losing their son and brother, they *do* know what they have, and they treasure one another and their merciful God, thanking Him for each precious day of life.

— Seventeen —

Praise Power

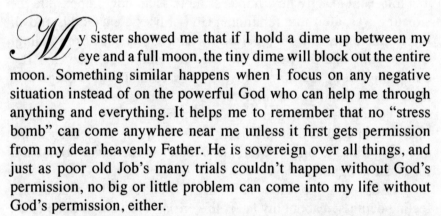

*M*y sister showed me that if I hold a dime up between my eye and a full moon, the tiny dime will block out the entire moon. Something similar happens when I focus on any negative situation instead of on the powerful God who can help me through anything and everything. It helps me to remember that no "stress bomb" can come anywhere near me unless it first gets permission from my dear heavenly Father. He is sovereign over all things, and just as poor old Job's many trials couldn't happen without God's permission, no big or little problem can come into my life without God's permission, either.

So, I'm trying to learn to remember that the ultimate question for me is "Will I trust God or not?" And the answer to every prayer I consider unanswered becomes, "Trust Me, Cathy. Just trust Me." It helps me to remember God would not even spare His own Son, but gave Him up for me, so how can I doubt He will always do what is best?

Once I heard a minister use a similar illustration I hope I never forget. He took a small box, about the size big enough to hold ten or twelve thank-you note cards, and held it up near his face. He said, "Imagine this box is my troubling situation right now. If I focus my eyes on this, I can't see anything else, and the box is enormous in my eyes. Yet if I turn my eyes up to God and praise Him, His greatness and power become my focus and this box shrinks down to its real size, which is miniscule compared to the Creator of all the galaxies."

His message helped me through a difficult time and I began a habit of singing praises to God every morning. My mother-in-law gave me a tiny book that spoke of the power there is in praising God. I learned over and over that when I sang praises *to* Him, instead of just singing *about* Him, my mind then focused on His greatness, size, power, faithfulness and all the wonders He has done. His greatness and enormity made the problems shrink, at least for a time, in my mind.

The same minister also shared the Old Testament story of King Jehoshaphat, who learned that savage tribes were about to attack him and his people who were vastly outnumbered. He turned to God and told Him exactly how hopeless he felt and how impossible the situation was, after first reminding God of how great God is and all the wonders He had done before — as if God needed reminding! But the king and the people *did* need to remind themselves. After consulting God, the king told the worship and praise singers to march in the front of the soldiers.

When the people began to praise and worship, the Lord defeated their enemies. They didn't even have to fight! God caused the attacking tribes to turn and kill one another so there was no one left for Israel to fight that day.

One day long ago I stood alone in my friend Jan's guest bedroom, feeling depressed about my latest life crisis. As an act of obedience, I began singing the scripture song, "In the day of trouble, He will hide me in His tabernacle; in the secret place of His tent He will hide me, and now my head will be lifted up above my enemies around me, and I will offer, in His tent, sacrifices with shouts of joy. I will sing, yes, I will sing praises to the Lord!"

The first time I sang it, I did not believe the words. I felt in that moment of discouragement as if God had not helped me. However, by the fourth time I sang the scripture, faith and hope rose up inside me and I knew for sure God was taking care of me, and He truly did have me hidden in the secret place in His tent, so nothing could ever permanently hurt me.

Since that day God trained me during various troubling times to turn my face and hands and voice up to Him in praise. Every time I did it, the change in my focus changed my thoughts, which changed my emotions from despair and darkness, to hope and life and trust and peace.

Before circumstances improved, my trust level always improved first. I realized maybe He was doing what I did as a young mom. Before I gave my son what he wanted, I told him to replace his whining with a polite request. God used these trials to train me to praise and trust Him more, before any change in circumstances happened. He has rescued me from every disaster and caused enormous good to come from each one.

There is still so much I do not know. One thing I do know: There is incredible, supernatural power in praising the Almighty God whose name is Jesus, and if we don't do it, the stones themselves will cry out!

— *Eighteen* —

Little Old Lady and Her Dog

~~>>◆<<~~

*S*he gazed into the mirror checking for new wrinkles and gray hair. *When did I become my mother?* she thought. Then, out loud, "I'm just a little old lady now, that's what I am."

Her husband smiled. "Yes, you are, Love, and I'm just your little old man, so come and give us a kiss." When Sarah made no move towards him, Timothy joined her at the mirror.

He wrapped his arms around her from behind and looked over her head, smiling until her smile matched his. "What did I ever do to deserve such a beautiful bride?" he asked.

"You did nothing, Love. Sure, 'tis the grace of God alone that gave us to each other those many years ago — and it's been His testing of us, too, at times! Can we really go to Florida next month, do you think?"

"We can, o' course. We've scrimped and saved, haven't we? That blasting sunshine will do us good. I'll turn as brown as a potato peel in the first two days. I can almost feel the glorious heat now."

"What about Rascal? He's not well and he needs me here."

"Sure, Maria and Sean will dote on him, so the creature won't even notice we're gone." Tim silently prayed his wife's seventeen-year-old dog would survive at least a little longer.

"All right, I'm praying, Timothy, and I do want to be there, it's just the journey itself I dread." Sarah asked God again to enable her to do all she needed to do before leaving their home in Cork City for two weeks.

The dark pit of depression had lured her recently, but so far she escaped the brunt of its tyranny. The relentless rain and damp chill of their disappointing Irish summer hadn't helped. Yet God's voice of truth still broke through and brought some sunshine on most days.

Yes, the Sunshine State of Florida, that's what we need. Once we get there it'll be hardly any expense at all because we can eat at the buffet restaurants for next to nothing, she thought. *And we can stay at Cassie's condo, sit by the pool and do a bit of people watching and pelican watching. Yes, Lord, please make it happen. I don't have the energy to get us ready, but if it's Your will, please just move me along like one of those suitcases on the conveyer belt at the airport.*

The night before their flight, she was still not sure she would actually make it. Her thoughts raced in circles, never getting anywhere, like guinea pigs in a cage. Yet, the next morning, they were packed and ready to go. She gave a last goodbye to her son Sean, her sister Maria and poor elderly Rascal. "Be good boys, now, and mind your Aunt Maria. Sean, if anything happens, you text me right away, do you hear?"

Sean said, "Absolutely, Mom," but over her head he saw his dad holding up his own phone and gesturing that it was *his* phone he should ring or text and not Sarah's.

When they arrived in Florida, Sarah radiated her excitement. "Cassie, it's nothing but a miracle we're here. As late as last night I was sure we wouldn't make it. I just couldn't cope with all the packing and the rest of it, but look, here we are. We made it! It's a miracle of the Lord."

The sound of Sarah's musical Irish accent lifted and warmed Cassie's heart as it always did. She and her family felt their Irish friends brought music to Florida with their lilting voices, and when they left, the music departed with them. Within minutes of their arrival, Tim and Sarah had her laughing, as always. They reminded her of comedy duos she watched in old movies on TV as a child — Abbot & Costello, Martin & Lewis. The duo of "Sarah and Tim" spread laughter everywhere they went.

The day after their arrival they all went "yard sale-ing" with Cassie's sisters. It amazed them the variety of brand-new treasures they could find, many with the original tags still on them. They found a sunflower pillowcase for their dear friend Rita back home and a giant phone-book-sized Sudoku book for Sarah's sister Ellen. They even found a water bowl for Maria's dogs — three small souvenirs already, on their first full day in Florida.

Yet, when they returned to Cassie's condo, disaster struck — the very thing they dreaded. Sarah was in the bathroom in the back bedroom when Tim cornered Cassie in the kitchen.

"The dog is dead. Sean texted me while we were shopping, but I don't want Sarah to know yet because I want her to have at least one day of rest before taking on this stress. Pray, pray for wisdom to know when to tell her the news."

Cassie did. She silently begged God to help her friend stay out of the pit of depression she had avoided for six whole years. She also prayed Sarah would learn the news at the perfect time.

The perfect time came immediately. She heard a desperate cry from the back bedroom.

"Timothy Crowley! When did you find out? Oh, I knew I shouldn't have left the poor dog alone there. Oh, no, Tim! Was Sean the only one with him? My poor son! Or was the poor dog alone when he died? He probably died from the stress of me leaving him. I'm the only one who can really comfort him. Oh, I knew I shouldn't leave him!"

Cassie's heart ached for her Irish friend. Tim tried to console and reassure Sarah, reminding her that the dog was seventeen years old and had suffered a long time. But Sarah would have none of it.

"He wasn't suffering! He stayed comfortable enough, even with all the ailments, as long as we made sure he only ate the one food that didn't give him the bloody diarrhea. What was I thinking? Why did I come here? I must go home, right now. Tim, call the airline, call them this minute. My poor dog and my poor son! What a thing to have to go through alone!"

Tim dialed his phone, but he stepped outside to do so. Cassie asked her friend if they might pray together and ask God for comfort and wisdom.

Cassie began as she often did, "Father God, we don't know how to pray, even the Bible says we don't. So will you pray through us by Your powerful Holy Spirit, something that will help poor Sarah?

Lord, her heart is broken. This is the thing she dreaded and feared the most. Help her, Jesus. You say You heal the brokenhearted and bind up their wounds. She feels desperate for that now, Lord. Be her Comforter and her Counselor and apply the precious ointment of Your love that only You can give."

When Cassie grew quiet, Sarah prayed. "Jesus, help me. The thing I fear most is for this to become a wedge between You and me and make me feel far away from You again. I want to feel near You, Jesus. You are the only One who can see into my heart and You are the only One who can help. Help me, Lord. Help me trust that You truly do *all* things well."

Sarah's breathing slowed and steadied and her sobs became less wrenching. The blank and lost look in her eyes was now replaced by a glimmer of life.

"Maybe it *was* for the best," she said. "Maybe the poor creature only held onto his miserable life for my sake. He might've wanted to leave us long ago and only stayed for me. It couldn't have been much of a life for him lately."

For the next four days, Sarah's face waxed and waned like the phases of the moon. For a while after each time of prayer with Timothy and Cassie, her eyes regained their light and she actually engaged with Cassie's family and played charades and other games with them after meals.

Speaking on the phone to her son and sisters back in Cork City confirmed to Sarah that God's timing was indeed perfect. Her son had handled the necessary trip to the vet like the brave young man he had become, and her sisters assured her it was all for the best and under no circumstance should she shorten her vacation.

On the day she first learned the news, Sarah needed several prayer breaks with her husband and friend to keep the light and life in her eyes and mind. The second and third days she needed only two. By the fourth day, her regular personal time of prayer carried her through the whole day. She marveled at God's ability to comfort her grieving heart. The bright Florida sunshine poured His love and healing into her and she almost felt guilty for not grieving more.

Sarah received another shock, a pleasant one, when she returned to Ireland. Instead of the empty house breaking her heart all over again, as she had dreaded, she found it a relief to not have to act as constant caregiver to an aged and ailing animal. She began a home business of caring for other people's pets when they went on vacations, which satisfied her love for animals but also gave her times of freedom from care.

Thank You, Lord, for giving Rascal so many years with our family. Thank You that all of them were good years for him until this last one. Thank You for Your mercy in sparing me the pain of having to watch him being put to sleep. Most of all, thank You for drawing me closer to You in my time of need and showing Me again how close You can be to the needy and heartbroken.

— *Nineteen* —

Goliath's Blessing

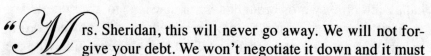

"*M*rs. Sheridan, this will never go away. We will not forgive your debt. We won't negotiate it down and it must be paid in full."

Hasn't she heard me? Rebecca thought. *I told her I'm paying her bank as much as I can every month. Does she think she can get blood from a turnip? I've told her I sold almost everything I have except my house so I can try to whittle away at her bank's loan and the rest of more than $100,000 I owe to fifteen different creditors. I rented out my house while I move around to live with friends and relatives. I did that so I'd have more to add to the monthly debt payments, and I told her all the debts were left to me as a farewell gift from my foolish, brief marriage to a talented conman.*

The attorney for the bank sat beside the bank's officer, Ms. Brooke. He must have been moved by a soft heart or by an angel whispering in his ear. He spoke, after several seconds of awkward silence.

"Mrs. Sheridan, your situation reminds me of my Grandmother's. When her husband died she, too, found herself overwhelmed by debt. Although I'll probably get in trouble with Ms. Brooke and her bank, I feel compelled to advise you to file for bankruptcy."

"No," Rebecca Sheridan said. "That is not an option. You can see, there on the list I gave you, all the debts and how much I'm paying on each one. As soon as I pay off another small one, I will, as I said before, add that amount to what I'm sending your bank."

63

"Mrs. Sheridan, usually in this type of meeting," the attorney said, "we see disorganized people who are looking for an escape. But the documents you prepared for us are the most organized I've ever seen in a situation like this."

Rebecca heard the phrase "most organized" and a spark of electricity went off in her brain. Becoming a more organized person was the elusive, impossible dream of her whole life. Usually she just gave up and didn't try. In high school she even had a contest with a friend to see whose notebook could become the messiest. This man uttered words which gave her hope that if she, Becky Sheridan, could be pronounced organized, surely *anything* was possible!

"The most organized I've ever seen in a situation like this." The happy jolt of his words brought a bit of sunshine to a very dark day. A sheriff's deputy had surprised her ninety days earlier by delivering to her front door a summons to appear at today's deposition with the bank and their lawyer.

For all of the ninety days, it had hung like a dark shadow over her life, but drove her to hours of prayer and preparation. Now it seemed God brought a blessing through the attorney's words, out of what—up to now—had been a giant curse of anxiety and shame.

The ray of sunshine was brief. The bank's representative, prim and proper, cold-hearted Ms. Brooke, repeated her firm position.

"The fact remains that your signature is on the loan and we will take whatever actions necessary to collect the full amount. Mrs. Sheridan, your debt is not going away and the amount you are sending each month is not acceptable."

The meeting ended after Becky said she would reduce the amount sent to two other loans by a few dollars each. This would allow her to send ten more dollars monthly to Ms. Brooke's bank.

Exiting the conference room, she saw her friend, Doris, seated in the waiting room. She had driven Becky to this meeting, prayed with her before the deposition and promised to continue praying through the whole ordeal. The first thing Rebecca said to her was, "Their attorney said I was organized!" Those unfamiliar words almost made going through the trauma worth it — almost.

What *did* make it worth it all was the experience of God's faithfulness she looked back on and shared with others going through a similar ordeal. Despite her foolish choices and their consequences, God came through for her as He always did. Thirty days after the deposition, she received a letter from the bank, offering to settle her debt for 40% of the original amount. Although the Goliath of debt didn't disappear, it shrank in size by 60%.

The intimidating giant of fear and dread *did* die on this day. Once again, God showed Himself strong on her behalf, and He caused all things to work together for her good as He promised in His Word. God enabled her to settle or pay off all her gargantuan debt within four years, and to re-establish an excellent credit rating within six years. Becky felt she would go through the misery again if necessary to gain the nearness and dearness of her intimate times with God, and learning once again how He can turn curses into blessings, even the curse of a Goliath.

— Twenty —

A Mouth Full of Laughter

$\mathcal{W}$orking with wedding photographs was my happy part-time job. I arranged them to tell the story of each wedding in album format for my friend who was one of the best photographers in town. From the getting-ready hair salon scenes to the final escape-to-the-limo excitement, it usually delighted me to work with these lovely symbols of happiness.

One day a photo, without warning, made my heart hurt and I gasped in pain. It showed the glowing middle-aged bride, standing with eyes and nose buried in her brilliant red rose bouquet. Behind her, over her shoulder, the elegant groom stood spying on her. He devoured her with the love in his eyes.

In that moment, the memory of my recent failed relationship came flooding back to me. It seemed a cruel irony that I had again given my heart to someone who found another woman he preferred. Feelings of self-pity and rejection, which I thought were healed, returned. I couldn't bear to look at the adoration in the gaze of the groom in this particular photograph. *Lord, why will no one ever look at me this way?* I whispered to God.

He answered with a glorious thought that came into my mind like sunshine breaking through dark black thunderclouds. *Someone does look at you this way, 24 hours a day, 7 days a week, always. I am enthralled by your beauty, and I am enraptured with love for you. You are the one for whom I suffered and died so we can be together forever. No woman has ever been loved more than this.*

My response poured out through tears of joy. *Oh, Jesus! Oh, Father God! Oh, precious, inside-me-always Holy Spirit of Almighty God, thank You for loving me so much! You didn't have to create me. You didn't have to die to save me, but You did. Thank You for loving on me just now.*

Only a few weeks before this day, I had read in Job 8:21, "He will yet fill your mouth with laughter and your lips with shouts of joy." I had struggled to believe I'd laugh and rejoice when even smiling seemed an impossible chore after the recent heartbreak. In spite of this, I had meditated on the verse and trusted God's promise. So the day my Heart Whisperer whispered His love to me in answer to my cry of loneliness in the photography shop, smiling came easily through the tears. He filled me with an indescribable love and assurance that warmed and filled my heart. A new season of laughter and joy began with this precious reminder of His endless desire for me.

My sisters and I began a weekly get-together with our only goal being to laugh until breathless. We've been achieving that goal for several years now and I often remember God's promise to fill my mouth with laughter during a time when I found it hard to even smile. He has given me more laughter in these past ten years than in all the years before.

Unless you've experienced the utter joy that comes from being freed by His grace, I don't know how to explain it to you, but I'll try. In the New International Version of the Bible, the disciple Peter calls it "an inexpressible and glorious joy" and in the King James Version, it's "joy unspeakable and full of glory."

Did you ever have a moment on a swing or amusement park ride when you felt as if you were flying? That's a glimpse of the kind of joy and freedom He gives me with His loving, encouraging, comforting words. Until He began to do this for me by the power of His Holy Spirit, no one had ever told me it was possible to have the God of all the universe whisper love songs and love notes to my heart. Yet each time He did it, I later saw a similar statement in the Bible, without even searching for it. It was as if He wanted to assure me these Holy Spirit-inspired thoughts truly came from Him. Here's an example of an early one right after I became a Christian.

I sat by a river praying for comfort at a time when my heart ached. I don't remember exactly what I prayed, but I know I felt miserable. As I sat looking at the river, a surprising thought came to my mind that I now know came from God. He told me to stop hating my body because of its imperfections, and that I was made exactly the way He wanted to make me. This shocked me, and I wanted to believe it, but it seemed too good to be true. Would God really talk to me about my hatred of my thighs?

That night during worship in our home-fellowship group, a young man read a scripture I had never heard, "I will give thanks to Thee, for I am fearfully and wonderfully made, and my soul knows it very well." He was excited about the verse and sang it to us and then taught us to sing along with him. What a joyful song, and it confirmed what the Lord had spoken to my heart that very day.

Another time, when I was feeling sick with worry for my huge family of parents, sisters, nieces and nephews, as if an ominous cloud was permanently assigned to us, the Lord spoke this to my heart: *When you think of your family, you feel a heaviness in your heart like a dark shadow of fear and worry about them, but that's a lie. What is over all of you is My banner of love, and this is what it says, "They are Mine, and they shall belong to no other."*

The chronic cloud lifted that day and has not returned, at least never for long. As the book of Proverbs promises, my path has become brighter and brighter, like the first light of dawn.

There have been many difficult moments and sometimes long hard seasons, but even on the darkest days, the promise that we are forever His has brightened the path. My Heart Whisperer knows how to encourage me, build me up and give me hope when things look hopeless. *Thank you, Jesus. You have truly, again and again, filled my mouth with laughter and my lips with shouts of joy.*

If you, dear reader, are a widow or divorced man or woman, or a lonely neglected spouse, He might be whispering to you right now. The Bible says He heals the brokenhearted and binds up their wounds. If you open His Word, read, and ask Him, you may hear Him. There is no other voice as loving as His, and He may have a mouth full of laughter waiting for you, too.

— *Twenty-One* —

Oil on My Head

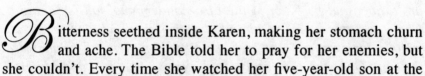

itterness seethed inside Karen, making her stomach churn and ache. The Bible told her to pray for her enemies, but she couldn't. Every time she watched her five-year-old son at the soccer field, she saw the object of her rage — a woman wearing skin-tight size-three jeans. This tiny woman had recently become stepmother to Karen's son, William.

"At least her *face* isn't gorgeous," she thought. "If she also had a beautiful face it would be the final straw. William loves her and her cooking, and I have to admit she's the best stepmom I've ever seen, but I wonder if that will last. How can I cope with this impossible situation?"

Karen's co-worker, Jaclyn, came and stood next to her. "Is that her?" she asked.

"Yep, she's the short one, with the tiny rear end, over there by the bench. Look, she's hugging William now."

"Who does she think she is?" Jaclyn said. "You're his mom, not her!"

"Yeah, I know, but she adores William, and the feeling is mutual. What else can I do but try to get along with her?"

"Do you want me to trip her when she walks by me?"

Karen chuckled at her friend who could always make her laugh. "No, but thanks, I'll just focus on the game."

That night at home after William was asleep, Karen sat down to pray. "Lord, I've avoided praying, because I know this bitterness in my heart is wrong and I've wanted to ask You to cause something painful to hurt her. I've enjoyed all these vindictive thoughts towards her and her husband — who used to be *my* husband! I know it's wrong, but You want honesty, don't You? And You already know everything anyway. You say in the Bible to hurl all our cares on You because You care for us, so I'm dumping all this ugly bitterness out for you to erase. I can't forgive, but I'm willing, so I ask You to please put forgiveness into my heart. I dread the rebuke I know I deserve, but I miss You, Lord, and I'm miserable with this inside me. I'll be quiet now and wait to hear You rebuke me."

Karen, I have no rebuke for you, for you've been walking in your own rebuke, and in that of the enemy of your soul. He's stirring you up to hate and be bitter, while also condemning you for doing it. I have a better way. I've already forgiven you and died to pay the penalty for every sin you ever committed or ever will commit. I'm the only One who can forgive and cleanse like this, and My Holy Spirit lives in you 24/7 and can make you able to forgive – for your own sake as much as for theirs.

Karen's heart softened when she heard God's sweet words, and tears flowed like melting wax from a candle, dissolving her bitterness. She knew God was the One who put these gentle and loving thoughts into her mind because her usual thoughts buzzed around like bees in her head! Yet when Jesus guided her into His truth, it always brought soothing peace and energizing joy.

A pen and note card beckoned from the table beside her. She wrote one of the most gracious notes of her life, an apology note for the cold-shouldering given to William's step-mother at the soccer games. It surprised her to see the words that flowed from her pen.

Since all three of William's "parents" now had the last name "Warren," she wrote: *Please forgive me as I continue to adjust to this "post-Warren" era in my life. It helps me to keep my distance from both of you while I heal, but I never want to cause hurt or offense to two people who are loved so much by William and by Jesus. I'm truly sorry for acting with rudeness toward you, and I hope we can cooperate as we parent William together.*

The burden God lifted while she prayed and wrote invigorated her more than a thirty-pound weight loss. She once again experienced

God to be more than all she needed. When she opened her Bible, she noticed these words in the book of Lamentations, "I remember my affliction and my wandering, the bitterness and the gall. I well remember them and my soul is downcast within me. But this I call to mind and therefore I have hope: because of the Lord's great love, we are not consumed, for His mercies never fail, His compassions never come to an end. They are new every morning. Great is Your faithfulness, O Lord."

Oh Jesus, You're so kind to me, she prayed. *No one loves as gently as You do, so please give me Your kind of grace and gentle love for other people. Even Your rebukes are gentler than my softest words!*

Long after the soccer field incident, she stumbled onto a verse explaining what she experienced with God's gentle corrections: "Let the Righteous One strike me, it is a kindness. Let Him rebuke me, it is like oil on my head. My head will not refuse it" (Psalms 141:5, NIV).

Jesus, You're my shepherd, and someone said Your anointing my head with oil accomplishes many things, including the protection a human shepherd puts on his sheep to keep pesky insects away. Thank you for protecting me when you put forgiveness in my heart. What a bitter, shriveled-up woman I could be right now if not for your miracle work in me.

Karen meditated on what Paul wrote in the New Testament about God's kingdom not being harsh rules, but instead consisting of righteousness, joy and peace in the Holy Spirit. She remembered a friend who leaped for joy one day and called it having a "bene-*fit*." She laughed and prayed aloud, "What an inheritance, what a kingdom, hallelujah! Pour on the oil, Lord!"

Twenty-Two

Home

*W*henever she needed to make a big decision, Rachel knew where to go. She drove until she found a quiet place where she could look at a body of water. Somehow the sight of water seemed to calm the agitated thoughts in her mind so she could listen for God's guidance that came from His gentle voice of peace. Today she drove to a bayou near the Day Center where she had just dropped off her elderly mom.

Lord, I'm thinking maybe You want me to move back here after this summer visit, she prayed. *I know they need me here to help take care of Mom. It's obvious I'm needed, but I need to hear from You. James won't move here with me, so I feel I'd be abandoning my teenager when he has one more year in high school. Both he and his dad encouraged me to make the move because they believe it's the right thing to do, but I need to know what You want me to do.*

Help me, Lord! Your Word says Your wisdom is pure, peaceable, reasonable, full of mercy and good fruit, unwavering and without hypocrisy. Give me Your wisdom, because my mind is wavering back and forth. Please whisper to me while I wait.

Rachel softly sang praise songs to God as she looked across the bayou to the bay beyond it. Her attention turned to a red cardinal landing on a tiny tree beside her. A sweet and gentle thought, so unlike her usual thought patterns, dropped into her mind and she recognized God's gentle whisper.

Rachel, watch this bird. It goes where I send it. Your home is not a geographical place, your home is Me. Move here and watch Me work through you. I will take care of James. He and his dad encouraged you to make the move and I am confirming it. Your home is in Me, in My will.

As she watched the red cardinal take off from the branch, she knew what she needed to do.

— *Twenty-Three* —

Fear Extinguisher

*H*e sat staring at the black box like a creature drugged and dulled by his need. The dark void inside him ached for an infilling of … something. He knew that keeping his eyes fixed on this mesmerizing box would prevent the sharp claws of fear from attacking his brain.

So he stared until sleep overtook him … comforting sleep, a type of slumber undisturbed even by daylight and his daytime work duties. Each night his faithful "box friend" renewed and restored the numbness of all his senses, as a protection against the unrelenting and unnamed creature with sharp painful talons and teeth.

His co-workers didn't guess what secretly haunted him. At times they noticed glassiness come over his eyes, but they thought he was just a daydreamer, "lost in his thoughts," they imagined.

So successful were his nightly numb-outs that the painful fears gradually reduced to only rare visits in nighttime dreams. *What a good life I have,* he thought. *Now for someone to share it!* Yet when he tried to neglect the black altar to meet up with other people, the claws of fear returned. "Not worth it, not worth it," he muttered to himself as he ran for home. He ran home to the safety of the black box and the endless, soothing numbness.

Late one night, when he lay in his bed and closed his eyes for physical sleep, an image he had watched on the black box tormented his thoughts. He knew why. The scene playing in his mind stirred up early, intimate memories long buried and denied. Memories of a long-ago betrayal and disturbing abuse he suffered as a child played over and over in his mind.

He considered returning to the black box, but feared seeing a similar image like the one that conjured up this long-ignored memory now torturing him. Those scenes of himself as a child being misused and afraid repeated in his mind until it felt his brain might shatter. This late night terror exceeded all other fears that chased him and he felt caught, desperate.

If this doesn't stop, it will kill me or drive me insane, he thought. In desperation and anguish he cried aloud in his empty room, "Jesus Christ, help me! Help me or I will die."

The disturbing scene in his mind changed. In its place he saw a very different image from his childhood. He saw Jesus as he'd looked in his Sunday School books and on the cover of his blue Bible, with children surrounding Him to be blessed and touched.

In his mind's eye, Jesus stood holding out His arms, offering a security and peace he had never known in his life. All the fear was gone, all of it. His heart and mind rested in powerful safety for which he had no name. Although he had attended church long ago, the true gospel now made sense to him for the first time.

This Jesus, he thought, *this Being who rescued me from madness when I called out to Him just now, took all the darkness and suffering my sins deserve and He is giving me life and light and peace and forgiveness in their place. He really, really loves me. He didn't do all that suffering just for the world. He did it for me, especially for me.*

He is my safe place and the One who has everything I need. He is the peace and the fear-extinguisher I have needed. Oh Jesus, thank You for rescuing me! Thank You that the monster of fear and shame who has chased and tormented me all my life has driven me straight into Your arms. Thank You for being the perfect friend and father and brother. I want everyone in the world to know You!

— *Twenty-Four* —

Feasting on Joy

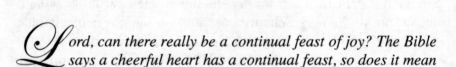

ord, can there really be a continual feast of joy? The Bible says a cheerful heart has a continual feast, so does it mean You want me to always be infused with Your joy?

In the gospel of John, Lord, You said You were telling us about Your love so Your joy would be in us and our joy would be full. I want that kind of joy to overflow from me onto people who are hurting and I'd like to help smooth out some of the worry creases on the foreheads of people I love. Can You fill me so full that I spill out some contagious joy?

Jesus, You've often kept Your promise to fill my mouth with laughter and my lips with shouts of joy, so would You make it more consistent? Will You transform this stone-hard heart of mine that often persists in selfishness? Will you please help me welcome everyone who interrupts me in my work today as an opportunity to give out Your grace and joy?

In the book of Psalms You tell us there's fullness of joy in Your presence, and in another chapter You say You set us in Your presence forever. So that sounds like continual joy to me.

Is that the continual feast — to be always mindful I'm in Your presence? My friend says joy is a gauge of our faith, and there are many days I know I've tried to run on empty. Don't let it happen today, Lord. Fill up my fuel tank, please.

Fill me with the fullness of faith and joy that can only come from Your Word, and keep me praising You all day long so I'll be sensitive to the slightest promptings from Your Holy Spirit.

I know no one cares much about what I know. But oh, how joy-hungry this world is, and You, Lord, are the fountain source, the Author and Creator of real joy. One of my favorite songs calls You the "well-spring of the joy of living."

And You invented laughter, Father God! I can't wait to hear You laugh in heaven. Will it sound like the thunderous roar of the lion I heard at the Wild Animal Park? Or will it remind me of each unique and precious laugh of everyone I love?

Thanks for giving us this priceless ability to laugh, and for the gift of Your inexpressible and glorious joy. Thank You for this delicious feast of joy here with You this morning — and it came with no calories and no grams of fat!

— *Twenty-Five* —

Anything Else

*T*wice in the same week two different friends told me of a woman who wrote Bible studies they thought I'd enjoy. I believe it was God who prompted them to recommend her to me, because her love for God resonated from every page. Each time I completed one of her studies, either alone or in a group, I brought a "take-away" of truth or insight that always stayed with me and helped me.

On one page of the workbook for one of her studies, she asked, "Who is someone you always feel sure really loves you?" I thought of all the family and friends God had blessed me with. Yet I couldn't help writing the name "Jesus" on the blank line beside the question. I didn't do it because it was the expected answer, since no one would read it but me. I wrote it because His love for me had gone deep into my bones for over twenty years and filled up places that no one and nothing else ever could.

However, I felt curious about other people's answers. So I asked someone who had the finest, most mature Christian husband I knew. He was the guy everyone wanted to have in their hospital waiting room during surgery or emergencies, because his very presence brought calm and reassurance. He is still one of the most faithful and dependable men most of us will ever know. Yet when I asked his wife whose name she wrote down as being someone she always felt sure really loved her, her answer surprised me.

She said, "I wrote 'Jesus,' because anything else hurts too much."

Wow! What a lesson she gave to me that day, and she probably doesn't even remember it. Don't you love it when God whispers to you through the most soft-spoken and gentle people you know?

I've shared her words with almost every Bible study group I've led since then. It can help all of us when we remember that other people can never satisfy our deepest needs and longings, at least not for long. This dear woman had learned not to expect fulfillment from anything else but Jesus, and it showed in the kind and loving life she lived. His love is the only one that never, ever lets us down. Anything else is only human.

— Twenty-Six —

A Fine Whine

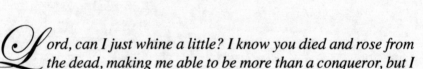

ord, can I just whine a little? I know you died and rose from the dead, making me able to be more than a conqueror, but I seem to keep doing some of the same stupid things again, like eating quickly and therefore eating way too much.

I thank You from the bottom of my heart for those fifty pounds You've helped me lose and keep off my body for more than four years now! Help me to never go back to the life of constant pig-outs every evening and thank You that those are no longer a frequent occurrence.

But Lord, recently I've reverted to the habit of eating so fast that it results in overeating. Help me just say no to excess of all kinds. Thank You that every day can be a fresh start with You. You told us in the gospel of Luke to watch out and be on guard against all kinds of greed, so please help me be greedy for nothing except for more of You!

And thank You for these four years of freedom from a life of eating mostly fast food and sodas. Even though the drive-through windows used to be my daily feeding troughs, they don't even tempt me anymore. Can you make all excess food become just as unappealing, or help me slow down so I'll eat half as much?

Give me more creative ideas to help in getting healthier and help me remember Your words are sweeter and more satisfying than any excess food. You really do feed me "with the finest of wheat and with honey from the Rock."

Use me now, Lord, to do powerful, fervent and effective praying for all the loved ones You've brought into my life. Thank You for each of these dear ones You've blessed me with, and for all Your endless mercy and grace poured out on me.

This fine whine has turned into a praise-a-thon, hasn't it? Well, that's Your doing, too, because from You and through You and to You are all things. To You be the glory forever!

Lessons

First, my Teacher taught me about His love for me.
Not a generic, one-size-fits-all-the-same love,
But an intimate knowing, specific affirmations,
Edification and consolations, a love that's even
More filling than warm chocolate lava cake.
This love flowed into ancient wounds and
Brokenness I didn't even know I had.

Often I asked for new lessons, but He seemed to say,
No, just this for now; you need to get this one deep in your bones.
And now I know why. Because when the earth moved
Under me and the mountains fell on my head,
I learned that nothing and no one can shake off
His love for me — His warm and filling and healing
Love for me. Whether or not it shows, He makes me
Feel like the radiant bride who stands with the light
Of her groom's love in her eyes.

Next, my Teacher taught me about His granite joy —
Stronger than fortresses, gravity or diamonds.
Joy that's stronger than grief, pain and woe.
Joy that strengthens me and bubbles up, sometimes,
Even in the depths of pain and suffering.

Now, He's teaching me His peace.
It used to be that thirty young children
Drained it all out of me on every workday.
But now, His love and His joy, those
First two lessons taught me, sometimes,
When I allow them to, flow out of me into the kids.
You should see our smiles.
Some days we have way too much fun!
His peace and His joy are like twins who appear together when
His love flows through a broken jar.

— Twenty-Seven —

A Teacher's Prayer

*J*essica gritted her teeth and repeated for what seemed like the thirtieth time, "No, Kenny, you do it *this* way." Poor Kenny. He had to struggle to focus on anything other than a computer monitor or TV screen. When he took a reading or math test on the computer he could get average scores, but in the world of paper and pencils and books, he consistently scored at least one year below his grade level. She prayed someday the state assessments would be available for him to take online.

She wanted to show more patience and compassion for Kenny and all her fourth-grade students. Many of them displayed blank stares when they should be listening. She joked with her family that if she didn't almost stand on her head she couldn't get their attention, much less teach them anything. She expressed her frustrations to God in prayer one night and asked Him to give her some new ideas or insight.

Jessica, forget about the progress and the goal until you first focus on each child. In the same way they're distracted by many things, so are you. Focus on making a real connection of love with each one of them.

More than knowledge, these particular students need love and focus from you. Remember what you read in My Word — knowledge can puff up or make arrogant, but love builds up. Build up your students by loving and focusing on them, and watch how they grow. You can have unseen effects on them that are eternal.

Make it your first priority to love them, and the progress will follow. Without the love, the progress will be hindered and you will be frustrated, so remember the three things that remain — faith, hope and love. Keep your attention on eternal things.

After writing down God's encouraging and challenging words in her prayer journal, Jessica slept the best and deepest sleep of the whole school year. The next day, as each child walked into her classroom, she made a point of making contact with every pair of eyes. Her patience increased when she remembered her first priority, trusting the progress to flow from that foundation of love and relationship.

She smiled to herself remembering how God continually educated *her* with His loving encouragement and not with forcing or pushing. Were the children more calm and focused today, or were they reflecting her inner progress?

That night, her mind wandered as she tried to read her Bible. She realized her wandering thoughts resembled a type of spiritual Attention Deficit Disorder. When she read the 22nd chapter of Proverbs she wrote "spiritual ADD" in the margin beside verses 17 and 18, "Pay attention and listen to the sayings of the wise; apply your heart to what I teach, for it is pleasing when you keep them in your heart and have all of them ready on your lips."

She copied the passage into her prayer journal. Then she prayed, "Lord, thank You for a new perspective on my most challenging students. Thank You for showing me again that talking with You brings peace, power, patience, perseverance and Your perspective about whatever circumstances surround me. Help me pay attention to You the way I want my students to pay attention to me, and please, Lord, keep me from having spiritual ADD!"

Twenty-Eight

Janet and Jonah

"Kay, I cannot move back to Florida. Why would God tell me to do that? I swore I'd never go back there, and if I did, I'd be sure to bump into my ex. It would kill me to see him with his new wife and children."

"How do you know God meant for you to move back to that small town? Did He specifically say move there?" Kay asked.

"No, the thought I keep hearing whispered in my mind is just 'Move to Florida.'"

"Well, Florida is a big state, so why don't you ask Him if some other place in Florida would be okay? Maybe you could come live near me!"

Janet hung up the phone. What a good idea her friend had given her! Maybe she could move to Tampa where her other friend Sharon lived. But when she prayed, she felt God wanted her to move to Orlando. *Ugh, I hate Orlando, Lord. Do I really have to move there? Well, at least I wouldn't bump into my ex, and I'd be very close to Kay, but I hate the thought of moving.*

For the next few weeks, Janet's mind struggled and worried. She often considered ignoring God's clear directions while she continued working the temporary jobs she'd begun after being laid off two months before. Yet each night before she fell asleep, she heard a gentle and firm whisper, "Move to Florida." One night she had a dream about the Bible story of Jonah ending up in the belly of a "great fish" after disobeying God.

85

The next morning she cried aloud to God, "Please help me, Jesus! I don't know how I can go through another move. I love it in Tennessee, so do I really have to move?"

She opened her Amplified Bible to the longest chapter in the whole Bible, Psalms 119. When she read the thirty-second verse, she knew it was for her. "I will run and not merely walk in the way of Your commands when You give me a heart that is willing."

Lord, please give me a willing heart. Thank You for providing everything I've needed even after I lost my job.

During the next few days, Janet noticed she actually felt excited about moving to Orlando. What a miracle! As she began to make all the arrangements, she even wondered what sweet blessings and assignments God might have in store for her in Florida. She had not really enjoyed the job she'd just lost here in Tennessee, so maybe she'd find a better one.

She read in the Bible that if she delighted herself in God, He would give her the desires of her heart. That would certainly be worth moving anywhere. She began to ask God to give her the desires of *His* heart, since the Bible said all the treasures of wisdom and knowledge are in Him.

Lord, how dare I think I know better than You do? Please forgive me and help me obey more quickly in the future. If You can change my heart this way, I know You can do anything else, too.

Just as she prepared to go, she got bad news from her mechanic. After a check-up to diagnose her car's strange new noises, he told her it needed major repairs that would cost more than the car was worth. When she took the car for a second opinion, the mechanic agreed with the first one. She called her friend in Florida.

"Kay, I only have enough money in my savings to get me to Florida to stay with you until I get another job, so I can't afford this."

"Let's pray," Kay said. "Father God Almighty, You are sovereign over moves and cars and jobs and everything else. You tell us the name of Jesus is above every other name and You say You give Your angels charge over us to guard us in all our ways, so in the powerful, unstoppable, unsurpassed name of Jesus, we ask You to send angels to get Janet to Florida by whatever means You provide.

Give her absolute peace about driving her car, Lord, if that is how You want her to get here. She is trusting You and You say those who trust You and keep their mind focused on You will have great peace. Thank You for all the ways You've been providing for her in these months without a steady job and thank You for this new opportunity to watch You prove again that You and You alone are her provider."

Janet put down the phone and *knew* that her car would make it all the way. Sure enough, she used it to move to Florida and also to drive fifty miles back and forth from Kay's home daily to job-hunt and apartment-hunt in Orlando for six weeks. Her old car lasted until she'd worked and saved money at her new job for almost a year.

Just as He promised, God began to fulfill the desires of Janet's heart when she made the choice to delight herself in Him. She grew in intimacy with her Savior and loved to tell people, in her soft and wonder-filled voice, "He's just *so* kind, so very, very kind." Never again did she consider following Jonah into the belly of a big fish!

— Twenty-Nine —

Do You Really?

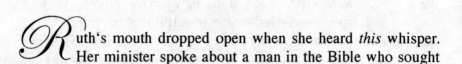

*R*uth's mouth dropped open when she heard *this* whisper. Her minister spoke about a man in the Bible who sought healing for many years and on many occasions. Jesus asked him a shocking question, "Do you want to get well?"

The same question had entered her mind as a gentle whisper. *Ruth, do you really want to get well?*

Well, of course I want to be healed. No one wants to suffer from illness! However, when she thought about it, she realized all the advantages the sickness offered her. It gave her an excuse for anything she didn't want to do and it had even become her identity. She thought about how often she discussed it, thought about it and analyzed it.

Lord, You say we are more than conquerors and we can do anything with Your strength and help. Forgive me for thinking of myself first as a sick person and secondly as Your daughter. Help me remember who and what You have made me. Your Word says You want to make me like a well-watered garden, like a spring whose waters never fail. It also says You always lead me in Your triumph.

After only thirty seconds of dwelling on the words of life God had whispered to her heart, Ruth knew she could make a choice. She could dwell on everything wrong in her life, or she could choose to dwell on everything "excellent and worthy of praise." In that moment, she began a new phase in her life, thanking and praising God for every blessing and even for life itself.

When the minister finished speaking, she joined in singing with all her heart a song about trading her sorrows, sickness, pain and shame in exchange for God's joy. Life didn't become perfect, but even colors around her in nature appeared more vibrant.

The illness radically improved, and on the most difficult days she meditated on these two scriptures: "I will bless the Lord at all times, His praise shall continually be in my mouth" and "He who sacrifices thank offerings honors Me and he prepares the way so that I may show him the salvation of God." Every time, focusing on truth and life lifted her spirits and eased her pain.

Thank You, Lord, for giving me a thankful heart. The more I don't feel like thanking and praising You, the more I know I need to do it. And every time I do, You show me Your saving power again and again. Thank You for making me Your daughter, and help me remember that's first and foremost what I am, bought with an incomparable price!

— Thirty —

Knowing

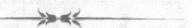

*S*ometimes God whispers to me through modern writers who love Jesus and His Word. In his book, *The Life You've Always Wanted*, John Ortberg taught me that every moment of my life is an opportunity to learn from Jesus. Often, especially in challenging moments, I remember this truth, and ask God to whisper His peacefulness and His wisdom to me. Ortberg's book also encouraged me to find a joy mentor, and to stop trying to be my own messiah! I've read his book at least ten times and been blessed every time.

Last summer another writer gave me several "take-away" ideas that helped me begin to achieve lifelong dreams. In her book, *Rising From Defeat-The Overcomer's Handbook*, Sherry Anderson gave me practical ways to increase helpful and productive habits while decreasing self-defeating ones. Since reading her book I've chosen to fast a few times from activities that robbed me of more fulfilling and creative pursuits. Her encouraging words inspired me to action and the actions brought results. As soon as I read these words in her introduction, I knew God had led me to her book:

With our human reasoning, we deduce that God expects some kind of victorious performance as we encounter challenges and trials in our lives. I found that I did not know God very well. He is not like I imagined Him to be. He is more loving, more powerful, more patient, more to be reverenced, more to be respected, and more awesome than I ever envisioned Him to be. It has been in getting to know Him that I have found the freedom to be myself, to be honest with Him, and to depend on His strength for everything.

I am learning about the grace of God. I have known for a long time what I should do, but could not do it. At times I've thought the Lord was disappointed in me because I had not done what I knew was His revealed will. But He knew I could not do it. He patiently waited while I made the discovery. The bottom line: I have found the secret of overcoming to be personal humility and the grace of God. "God resists the proud and gives grace to the humble."

Those words confirmed what God had been teaching me for almost thirty years. It reflected my own experience that when she got to *know* God, she discovered He was not like she "imagined Him to be." Just as I don't really know any of the celebrities I've heard about during most of my life, I don't really know God at all until I spend time with Him and listen to Him speak with me. Hearing and learning about Him are not the same thing as hearing and learning *from* Him. No matter how much someone tells me about another person, I'll never know him or her if we don't have times of communication together.

Fortunately, God left us a huge and fascinating book to guide the way. It's been a best-seller for many years. If we come to a section in the Bible that puts us to sleep, we can pray for help! I've realized what I considered boring details in the Old Testament can remind me that my Heavenly Father is attentive to details of building tents and temples. So, how much more attentive is He to building my life and character and future as I cooperate with Him?

Before we begin reading in the Bible each day, we can pray for God's guidance to know which book within the Bible is most relevant to the current situations facing us and our loved ones. The One who wrote the book also created our hearts, and He knows which page or verse or concept He wants to use to guide us each day.

Rereading the book of Proverbs each month has helped me for more than two decades. Since it's the book within the Bible that's most focused on God's wisdom, I'm hoping as I meditate on its truth it will keep me from repeating past mistakes.

There are 31 short chapters in the book of Proverbs, so there's one for each day of the month. Whenever it warns of staying away from "the adulterous woman," I understand it's also warning me from letting anything get between me and my Bridegroom. From unfortunate experiences, I've learned the emptiness and turmoil that come from wandering far from *His* arms.

Several statements in *Rising from Defeat* made me aware of complacency and passivity in my life, but instead of feeling condemned, I became excited about entering a new, more adventurous lifestyle. Although I hadn't neglected prayer and Bible reading, I had slipped into doing only the one-way side of the process instead of waiting to hear from God. This early morning time had become more of a religious ritual instead of true communication. During urgent situations I waited to listen for whispers, but on ordinary days I tended to go on "auto-pilot" instead of waiting to receive power and guidance for the day ahead.

Since God had often urged me to write a book to encourage people to "let Him love on them," I was pleased to see that another writer had used similar phrasing to describe His touch. Sherry Anderson wrote a declaration or affirmation on page 155 of her *Rising From Defeat*.

I renounce religion. Lord, I will meet with You daily, on purpose, and there will be a convergence. You are coming to the meeting, and I am coming, and there is going to be an exchange. I will give You my burdens and cast my cares on You, and You are just going to love on me. And You may even share something that is on Your heart with me. There is going to be a transformation when I meet with You, and a transfer. It is not that I just say my prayers; there is something that really happens. I declare You are going to lead me and guide me.

What she meant by "I renounce religion" is exactly what I needed to do. Instead of reading and praying as a religious ritual, I returned to an intimate daily time of true relationship-building. A minister I know often says religions are man's attempt to seek God, while the true good news of Christianity is God reaching down to bring man to Himself through Jesus. He also says religions tell us "do, do, do" while Jesus says, "It's done." He paid the price so we don't have to perform any rituals to try to reach Him. We can enter into intimate relationship with a real Person who loves us as no one else ever can.

Jesus confirmed this truth in John 17:3, my favorite verse of the Bible. He was praying to His Father in heaven and when He mentioned eternal life, He then gave a definition that thrilled my heart the first time I read it. In this moment of typing these words my heart is again thrilled by what He said.

"Now *this* is eternal life; that they may *know* You, the only true God, and Jesus Christ, whom You have sent." Wow! The eternal life begins right now, the minute we begin to *know* God, whose first name is Jesus. When we repent of our sins and ask for His forgiveness and lordship, we immediately begin eternal life! Knowing Him and being in intimate relationship with Him makes every other relationship and experience in life more meaningful and more joyful and even more "survivable" in the difficult moments. For me, the promise of being with Him forever in heaven is the icing on the cake, the graduation prize. It takes away the fear and dread of death because I intimately know the One who is waiting to welcome me afterwards.

When Paul wrote that he pressed on to attain the thing for which Christ died, I believe he meant pressing on to know God! It was for the purpose of making us right with God that Jesus died. He sent Jesus to die to pay for our sins so we can be God's adopted children. Paul wrote in his letter to Philippian Christians: "I consider everything a loss compared to the surpassing greatness of *knowing* Christ Jesus my Lord…I want to *know* Christ and the power of His resurrection…I press on toward the goal to win the prize for which God has called me heavenward in Christ Jesus."

Oh, dear reader, don't you want to *know* the One who made your precious heart? There were many years when I might've said I knew Him, but now I realize I only knew about Him. Once He began to whisper to my heart those "sweet somethings" that healed and filled and thrilled me, then I began to really know Him. The more I know Him, the more I want to know Him even more. Oh, how He loves us so!

— *Thirty-One* —

The Only Place

*C*harli is my joy mentor. She and I can even laugh together for no apparent reason. We were doing this after church one day when a mutual friend walked up and asked us what we were laughing about. Neither of us knew.

Charli has her share of reasons to be *joyless*. Her list of issues and challenges is no shorter than anyone else's and longer than many. But she has some secrets she has shared with me.

In her house she has a special small room where she meets with God every day. She keeps Bibles and journals handy and a comfortable chair, lamp and table. She tells Jesus all her troubles and concerns, worships Him and waits for Him to comfort her and give her joy and peace in exchange for any burden of discouragement, worry, or resentment.

Since she's been married almost fifty years, I sometimes ask her for secrets of their success. She always smiles a special, knowing smile and her face takes on a look of reminiscing. She tells me surviving and thriving in marriage has taught her many things about herself and about walking with Jesus. In her early days of marriage, before she knew Jesus, she stayed constantly dissatisfied and demanding of her husband and children.

However, she said when Jesus taught her how to get her deepest needs met by Him, and that He was the only One who could fill up the God-sized hole in the human heart, she found real joy and peace. She began to accept her husband and appreciate the many desirable and admirable qualities he had, instead of focusing on things she could not change. Just as God accepted and loved her with all her imperfections, she began to love and accept her children and husband just as they were.

An amazing thing happened. Her love *and* desire for her husband increased over the years! Through many changes and challenges and heartbreaks, they weathered every storm together. She wrote a poem to him after forty years of marriage saying her heart for him was "the place that never changes."

When she let me read her poem, my thoughts went to her special prayer room. I thought about all the changes we'd both seen in our lives, the good and the bad ones. Her prayer room symbolized for me my own "place that never changes."

The heart of Jesus for each of us, His love and companionship, His forgiveness and acceptance, His mercy and grace, these are the unchangeable and unfailing things. Fellowshipping with His heart is the place that never changes. It's the only place that can empower us to love and forgive with His kind of unconditional love and mercy and grace.

— *Thirty-Two* —

Dream Snatcher

⟫⟪

*A*s I walked in the brisk early morning, my forehead grew furrowed in spite of the inspiring music in my earphones. I couldn't stop worrying. *Lord, I can't finish this book. I'm the worst writer ever. If I go through with this, I'll humiliate myself and everyone who loves me. What was I thinking? There are so many "what if's?" I can't even begin to list them.*

My thoughts wouldn't calm down enough for me to hear any whispers at first. My hamster of a brain kept sprinting around and around in its cage. But I praised God for a moment, and then two words popped into my thoughts — *Dream Snatcher.*

Father God, is that You? For the first time in my life, I thought God laughed at me — not the mean kind of laughter, but the kind we can only do with our dearest ones who know how to tease without hurting.

He seemed to whisper, *Of course, Cathy. I told you to write the book to encourage people to let Me love on them. You only need to obey. Don't let anyone or anything snatch away your dream.*

Yes! How could I let doubts deprive me of the dream God had whispered to my heart? *I will not be denied,* I told myself. My flustered thoughts settled down and I remembered the words my brother-in-law left on a voicemail message after he prayed for the book. "Cathy, don't drop this. Don't let this fall to the ground."

Later, his daughter, my dear constant encourager, said, "These stories can help people. Everyone needs help with their heart at one time or another, and we know Who and how they can get it cleaned and healed for eternity. Put your stories out there and leave the rest to God."

End Notes/References

Looking Up – Hebrews 12:2; Colossians 3:1-2

Just Sit There – John 15:5, Galatians 2:20

Now or Never – Psalms 34:1; Psalms 50:23; Romans 8:28; 2 Samuel 12:19-24; Job 13:15

The Yellow Leaf – Luke 10:41-42; Psalms 86:7; Psalms 91:5; Isaiah 30:19; Isaiah 65:24; John 10:27

A New Name – Psalms 25:14; Isaiah 62:2; Isaiah 65:15; Colossians 1:29; 2 Corinthians 3:18; Romans 12:2; Philippians 12:13

Granite Joy – Nehemiah 8:10; John 15:5; Romans 8:28; Galatians 5:1; John 8:32, 36; Psalms 50:23; Matthew 11:29

ABC's – John 15:5, Isaiah 26:3; Psalms 23, Luke 10:41-42; Matthew 22:37-40; Galatians 5:22; Ephesians 5:9; Psalms 69:9

No Matter What – Matthew 22:37-40; Matthew 10:26; Romans 12:19; Proverbs 15:1; Colossians 3:13-14; Hebrews 12:15; 1 Peter 2:23

Combat Boot – Isaiah 54:10; Psalms 34:19

Heart Whisperer – Matthew 10:30; Luke 12:7; Philippians 3:9;
Philippians 4:19; Isaiah 65:24; Jeremiah 33:3; Psalms 56:3;
Psalms 34:19; Jeremiah 29:11-14; Romans 8:32; 2 Corinthians
5:21; Romans 1:17

Choice – Ephesians 2:14; Psalms 119:165; Galatians 5:22-23;
Philippians 4:6-7; Isaiah 26:3

April's Story – 2 Timothy 1:7; Romans 8:15; John 3:16-17; 1 Peter
1:8; Romans 10:9-10

April Continues – Philippians 4:13; Jeremiah 29:11; Isaiah 55:8;
Isaiah 61:3; Psalms 136:1-9; Romans 10:9-10

Ultimate Survivor – John 3:16-17; Philippians 4:13; 2 Peter 1:3-4;
Psalms 63:5; Proverbs 15:15

Diagnosis – Romans 15:13,4; Hebrews 6:19; Acts 2:26;
Romans 4:18; Romans 5:1-11; Romans 8:20-25; Romans
12:12; 2 Corinthians 1:7; Ephesians 1:18; Colossians 1:5; 1
Thessalonians 4:13

The Secret Place – Psalms 91; Ephesians 6:10-18; Jeremiah 17:14;
Matthew 10:1, 8; Acts 4:30; Malachi 4:2; Romans 10:17

Hospital Trauma – Romans 8:28; Psalms 91:11

Praise Power – Psalms 34:1; Psalms 63:5; Luke 19:40; Job 1:12;
Job 2:6; 2 Chronicles 20:18-22; Psalms 27:5-6; Isaiah 26:3;
Romans 8:32

Little Old Lady – Psalms 31:15; Ecclesiastes 3:1-8; Psalms 147:3;
Romans 8:26

Goliath's Blessing – Romans 8:28; Numbers 22:12; 1 Samuel
17:23-50; 2 Corinthians 8:2

Mouth Full of Laughter – Job 8:21; Psalms 45:11; 1 Peter 1:8; Song of Songs 2:4; Ezekiel 11:20; Malachi 3:17; Proverbs 4:18

Oil on My Head – Matthew 18:21-22; Mark 11:25; Psalms 141:5; Psalms 23:5; Romans 14:17; Colossians 3:13-14; Galatians 5:1; Romans 8:28; Hebrews 12:15; Lamentations 3:19-25

Home – James 3:17; James 3:5; Proverbs 3:5; Acts 17:28-29; John 15:4

Fear Extinguisher – John 3:16-17; 1 Timothy 1:7; Galatians 1:4; Romans 10:9-10

Feasting on Joy – Proverbs 15:15; Psalms 63:5; Galatians 5:22; John 15:11; 1 John 1:4; 1 Peter 1:8; Romans 10:17

Anything Else – Proverbs 20:6; Proverbs 19:22; Psalms 13:5; Psalms 26:3; Psalms 33:18; Psalms 90:14; Psalms 94:18; Romans 8:38-39

A Fine Whine – Lamentations 3:22-23; Psalms 119:103; Romans 11:36; Romans 8:37; Luke 12:15; Psalms 81:16; Psalms 147:14; Philippians 4:4-9

Lessons – Galatians 5:22-23; 1 Peter 1:8; Philippians 4:4-9; Romans 1:8b

A Teacher's Prayer – Proverbs 22:17-18; 1 Corinthians 13:1-13; 1 Corinthians 8:1b

Janet and Jonah – Psalms 37:4; Jonah 1:17; Psalms 91:11; Philippians 2:9; Isaiah 65:2, 24

Do You Really? – John 5:6; Isaiah 58:11; Romans 8:37; Philippians 4:8; Philippians 4:13; Psalms 50:23; Psalms 34:1; Psalms 52:8

Knowing – James 4:6; 1 Peter 5:5; Philippians 3:1, 4:4; 1 Thessalonians 5:16; Jude 1:24; 1 John 1:4; Acts 2:28; John 17:3; John 17:13; John 15:11; John 16:11; Jeremiah 29:11-14

Anderson, Sherry. *Rising From Defeat*. Maitland, Florida: Xulon Press, 2012.

Ortberg, John. *The Life You've Always Wanted*. Grand Rapids, Michigan: Zondervan Publishing House, 1998.

The Only Place – Philippians 4:8; 2 Corinthians 1:3-5; 1 Peter 1:8; 1 Corinthians 13:1-13; Isaiah 61:3

Dream Snatcher – Jeremiah 29:11; Proverbs 21:30; Psalms 103:13; Psalms 40:10-11; Psalms 42:8; Romans 8:38

CPSIA information can be obtained at www.ICGtesting.com
Printed in the USA
LVOW12s0304140913

352388LV00002B/117/P